Fabric Embellishing
The basics & beyond

Ruth Chandler
Liz Kettle
Heather Thomas
Lauren Vlcek

Fabric Embellishing
The basics & beyond

Ruth Chandler • Liz Kettle • Heather Thomas • Lauren Vlcek

Copyright© 2009 by Landauer Publishing, LLC

Fabric Embellishing The basics & beyond
Project Designs Copyright© 2009 by Ruth Chandler, Liz Kettle,
Heather Thomas, Lauren Vlcek

This book was designed, produced, and published by Landauer Publishing, LLC
3100 101st Street, Urbandale, IA 50322
www.landauercorp.com   800/557-2144

President/Publisher: Jeramy Lanigan Landauer
Vice President of Sales and Operations: Kitty Jacobson
Project Manager: Marjon Schaefer
Managing Editor: Jeri Simon
Art Director: Laurel Albright
Photographer: Sue Voegtlin

ISBN 13: 978-0-9818040-3-3
ISBN 10:   0-9818040-3-9

Library of Congress
Control Number: 2009927744

This book printed on
acid-free paper.
Printed in China

10-9-8-7-6-5-4-3

introduction

This book on embellishing is more than a collection of techniques—it is also the story of four artists who share a passion for fabric, art and fun stuff. As you look through the pages you will see four distinct styles and personalities and you may notice where we have influenced and borrowed from each other. We believe adding embellishments is more than just fun. It is a way for each of us to place our unique handprint on our creations. Embellishments help tell our personal story and reveal our personality and style. We won't lie to you though; the best part of embellishing is that we get to collect all sorts of cool and funky bits and pieces. Whether you are a traditional, contemporary or art fiber fanatic, within these pages you will find techniques to help you develop your skills, fill your toolbox and ignite your imagination. We developed this book to encourage experimentation and play and creating a technique workbook is a great way to try new embellishments and craft your own personal idea reference book. We want you to dive into the techniques, give them a try and make them your own. What are you waiting for? Go play!

Liz, Ruth, Heather & Lauren

"Let the boundaries we have learned as adults melt away and be replaced with creativity and imagination."

Ruth Chandler

table of contents

table of contents

Getting Started

Some people choose to read a how-to book from beginning to end to familiarize themselves with the contents and then decide which technique they'd like to try. Others dive right in, pick and practice a technique, and use it on their next piece. Whichever your approach, you end up with try-outs, test pieces and practice bits. We decided it would be fun to actually use those pieces to create a sample book—and the fabric technique workbook was born.

One way to learn is to tackle one technique a week; in a year's time you will have practiced all techniques in this book and own a workbook to refer to time and time again for inspiration. Even if you never use half of the techniques ever again, you'll have a beautiful record of your efforts. Get together with your friends, organize an embellishing group, and have weekly technique workshops.You will benefit from the creative synergy and save money by sharing and co-op purchasing supplies and tools.

Do you need to make a fabric workbook? Of course not! We do, however, encourage you to try every technique in this book, even if it falls outside your comfort zone—your experiments will lead your creativity to surprising results.

Just about every technique in this book features a large photo of the finished fabric workbook page. This fabric workbook page highlights the particular technique and is then further embellished and finished to be a stand-alone mini or journal quilt. The main technique is explained in a step-by-step sequence, with most steps accompanied by a photograph or illustration. The additional embellishment techniques are mentioned below the main photograph of the fabric workbook page.

Flaming Fabric
edge burning

This is a wonderful technique to use on art quilts, either directly on the edge of the quilt itself or on a quilted block which is then placed on top of a background. The look can be very old fashioned or quite contemporary.

Techniques: Burning, Stamping, Iron-on Crystals, Buttons

Every technique has a supply list with specific tools and materials you need for practicing the technique. The supply list does not mention the tools and materials needed for further embellishing the workbook page as these are specified within their own technique section.

Generally, the supply list does not mention the standard supplies that repeat throughout the book, such as fabric, sewing machine, cutting mat, etc. For information on these items go to page 10, General Supplies & Equipment.

supplies

- Quilted piece made with cotton or other natural fabrics, thin 100% cotton batting and cotton thread.

- Cigarette lighter—if possible choose one without a child safety feature.

- Old cotton towel and an old cotton wash cloth.

The Gallery pages, sprinkled throughout the book to admire and inspire, feature our work and show close-ups of embellishing techniques.

Sometimes a technique on the gallery piece matches the technique in that section, other times, they're placed randomly.

designer's gallery

Green Fairy
10 x 14 inches
Lauren Vlcek

Deconstructed Crazy Quilting
Making a Frame
Machine Embroidery
Couching
Printing Images
Beading Sequins

SAFETY PRECAUTIONS

The burning, melting and heating techniques need good ventilation, especially when using synthetic fabrics such as Tyvec and Lutradur. Also use ventilation when using discharge products such as bleach. We recommend wearing a respirator. If possible, wait for a nice day, get a long extension cord for your tools, and take it outside.

Wear eye-protection goggles. They keep your eyes safe when sewing through metal or when using liquids that can splash up in your face, such as bleach.

Disclaimer of Liability: Every effort has been made to ensure that all information in this book is accurate. However, due to individual skills, variations in equipment and supplies, and differences in conditions, the publisher cannot assume any responsibility for injuries, losses or other damages to property or persons that may result from use of the information presented in this book.

Each technique workbook page is an 8 x 10-inch journal quilt that highlights one main embellishing technique and then showcases a few other techniques of your choice. Working on a small scale may take some getting used to but it is the perfect size for exploring ideas, learning new techniques and experimenting with form or color without a big investment of time or materials but, ultimately, this is your workbook so feel free to work in any size or shape you wish.

1 The workbook page consists of a base fabric, batting, stabilizer and fabric backing. Some techniques work best with the batting underneath the fabric; other techniques work best with the batting and the stabilizer underneath the fabric. In most cases it is best to save the fabric backing until you're ready to apply the edge finish so your page will have a clean back.

2 Pick an embellishing technique that intrigues your muse or begin at the beginning, then play and explore to your heart's content. Cut your base fabric to the desired size. Depending on the chosen technique, the entire 8 x 10-inch base fabric is used or the surface is divided as shown in the diagrams below:

3 Once finished, layer your embellished page with batting and/or stabilizer (if not already attached) and backing fabric. The easiest edge finish for your fabric workbook page is a simple straight or zigzag stitch; however, it can be a lot of fun to try out different stitches or traditional quilt-binding techniques, or to add ribbon, rickrack, torn fabric strips or beads. There are no other rules here except to have fun.

4 For easy binder-ring assembly, choose either an eyelet or a tab-and-eyelet finish; either finish allows you to add additional pages as you learn and play with new techniques. For consistent placement of the binding holes make a template out of template plastic, stabilizer or heavy paper. Make small round or ¼-inch-long buttonholes or use grommets or eyelets.

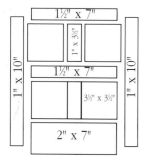

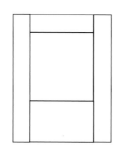

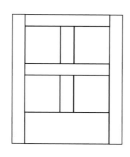

GROMMETS AND EYELETS DIRECTLY IN THE PAGE:

5 Grommets and eyelets differ in their construction but serve the same purpose—they reinforce the holes in your fabric workbook page. Grommets consist of two pieces and eyelets are one piece. Grommets are a bit sturdier but setting eyelets is a slightly easier process. Either will work well for your workbook and is very simple to use. We have found the Crop-A-Dile eyelet-setting tool to be the easiest method for setting eyelets in the fabric layers; however, it is costlier than simple grommet and eyelet setting tools. We recommend you refer to the instructions that come with each tool.

GROMMETS AND EYELETS IN TABS:

6 Cut two 3½-inch fabric squares and two 3½-inch squares of lightweight fusible interfacing and use a buttonhole foot or grommets or eyelets. Fuse the interfacing to the wrong side of each fabric square. It is important to use a lightweight interfacing because anything heavier makes turning the tab really difficult.

7 Fold the fabric square in half with right sides together. Sew around the raw edges using roughly a ⅛-inch seam allowance, leaving a 1-inch opening for turning along the long edge. NOTE: It is not necessary to sew along the long folded edge. Clip the corners, turn and press.

8 With short edges together, fold and pin the rectangle in half. Center a vertical buttonhole, grommet or eyelet ½ inch away from the fold. Making the buttonhole BEFORE the tab is sewn to the page is much easier since all of the bulk of the page is not interfering with the buttonhole foot on the sewing machine. The tab may look a little flappy at this point but, when sewn to the workbook page, it all comes together.

9 Pin the tab ends to the left edge of the fabric workbook page, centered about 1½ inches from the top or bottom, effectively inserting the edge of the page between the two halves of the tab.

10 To secure the tab to the workbook page, sew all the way around the tab about 1⁄16 inch inside the tab edges.

11 Bind the workbook pages together with metal binder rings from an office supply store or put them together by threading a funky ribbon through all of the button holes and tying a knot or a bow.

12 If desired, decorate the binder rings with ribbons, fabric strips or trims.

SEWING MACHINE & NEEDLES

A basic sewing machine is all you need for the embellishing techniques found in this book. A machine with a variety of programmed stitches is fun to have but not necessary; it is more important to have a clean and well-oiled machine than one with bells and whistles. It is helpful to have a needle down option and to be able to cover or drop the feed dogs.

Much of your fabric play can be done using basic sewing machine needles but adding quilting, embroidery, metallic and topstitch needles to your supply may be worthwhile as they are designed to protect delicate threads while sewing. Gather an assortment, including larger sizes which allow you to use thicker threads and sew through chunky materials.

Hand sewing, quilting and embroidery needles are made by many different manufacturers and most people have their preferred brands. We recommend you purchase quality needles as bargain needles tend to dull and bend quickly. Needles with a gold eye are often easier to thread; needle threaders are wonderful helpers with the, sometimes difficult, threading task.

CUTTING TOOLS

Rotary cutters, rulers and cutting mats make measuring and cutting fabric an easy chore. Sharp scissors make your work easier—we recommend at least a small and a large pair.

LIQUID & DRY ADHESIVES

Attach embellishment A to base B sounds easy but just how do we attach it and with which product? A wealth of liquid and dry (fusible webs) glue choices may leave us overwhelmed and confused so let's break it down. Your first decision is liquid or dry adhesion. Generally, we choose liquid glues when adding dimensional objects and dry adhesives for adding flat embellishments.

There are many wonderful liquid craft glues on the market and most brands work well. However, when working on fabric keep in mind two very important considerations: clear drying and flexible. Some of our favorite brands are Dries Clear Fabric Glue, TonerTex Fabric Adhesive, Aleene's Tacky Glue, Crafter's Pick The Ultimate and Crafter's Pick Incredibly Tacky. It is always a good idea to try new glues on a sample before using it on your work.

Dry adhesives, or fusible webs, are strands of glue formed into a fabric that, when heated, glue together two flat objects. Many brands and varieties are available but all work on the same principle and use an iron to activate the glue. Most of the products are interchangeable but some are heavier than others and will change the hand of your fabric.

The lightest weight fusible web products are Misty Fuse, Fine Fuse and Stitch Witchery. These lightweight products do not have a backing paper so a non-stick craft sheet, such as a Teflon sheet, is helpful to avoid getting the product on your iron. Lightweight fusibles are very helpful when using lightweight fabrics and products such as Angelina and Textiva.

There are many medium-weight fusible webs, such as Steam-A-Seam 2, regular and Lite, Wonder-Under and HeatnBond Lite. These products have a release paper on one or both sides. Some are tacky and temporarily adhere to your fabric until they are heat-bonded.

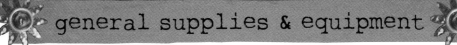

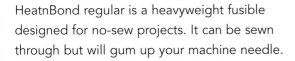

HeatnBond regular is a heavyweight fusible designed for no-sew projects. It can be sewn through but will gum up your machine needle.

Refer to the manufacturer's directions on the product as each one has specific directions and recommends different temperatures and steam or no steam settings on your iron. NOTE: Never place your iron directly on a fusible web because it will melt the web onto the sole plate. If this happens, use an iron cleaner or rub the sole plate on a fabric scrap until clean.

FABRICS AND THREADS

We love fabric and stand firmly on the side of 'the more the merrier.' Why limit yourself to only using cotton when an incredible variety of sheers, silks, polyesters, linens and bamboo fabrics is available? Also, vintage linens and garments supply us with wonderful fabrics, bits and buttons to use in our work. Last but not least, use your stash of ugly fabrics for trying-until-you-get-it-right or be pleasantly surprised with the effect of the technique on the fabric.

The 'more the merrier' philosophy applies to thread, too. There are so many exciting threads available, from ultra-fine polyester threads to big chunky hand-sewing threads; we love them all. Experiment to discover your favorites.

BATTING AND STABILIZERS

We do not have a preferred batting for making our workbook pages as the small size of the pages lends itself to using batting scraps leftover from other projects.

Stabilizers help control fabric distortion and they support, or even replace, fabrics when adding stitching or embellishments. A basic rule of thumb is the more you want to add on top of your fabric, the heavier the stabilizer needs to be.

Tear-Away Stabilizers: These stabilizers are meant to reinforce a fabric from the back and are torn away after stitching but, if necessary, they may be left attached. Common brands are Pellon Stitch-N-Tear, Sulky Tear-Easy and Sulky Totally Stable.

Cut-Away Stabilizers: Cut Away stabilizers are applied to the back of the fabric and are left in place after stitching or embellishment after cutting away the excess from the stitched or embellished area. Brands include Pellon, OESD and Sulky.

Interfacings: Made for garment construction, interfacings make great stabilizers and are often fusible on one side. They are especially useful for stabilizing unruly fabrics such as silks and satins. Many brands are readily available.

Heavyweight Stabilizers: Heavyweight stabilizers are very helpful when you want a stiff base for your project and are commonly used when creating fabric postcards, bowls and books. They vary from thin heavyweight to a thicker, padded heavyweight. Common brands are Pellon Ultra Heavyweight and Peltex 70, 71 and 72, Timtex and Lacy's Stiff Stuff.

Water-Soluble Stabilizers: The most common use of water-soluble stabilizers is in making free-motion thread lace embroidery. The stabilizer washes away completely or partially when soaked in water. They are also useful when leaving a stabilizer on the back would be undesirable such as when embellishing delicate fabrics. Common brands are Sulky and OESD.

foundations

Creating with embellishments can be somewhat overwhelming. Just where does one begin? How much is too little or too much? Each of us has our own unique design perspective so there is no right or wrong way to approach embellishing. Each technique is intriguing as a solo element or techniques can be used in combinations to create a symphony of delight. We like to think of embellishments as layers we add to our projects to help tell our personal stories. A great method for beginners is to choose one technique from each chapter and layer them from the foundation up.

Our 'foundation' techniques add style to clothing and purses, home décor and quilts. They shine on their own or make a great base layer for further embellishments. This important foundation supports the remaining layers physically as well as visually. Base fabrics are often ignored and neglected but they won't be relegated to an afterthought any longer. In this section we feature more than a dozen awesome ways to embellish our base fabric as we add imagery, use scraps, scrunch, bubble, tuck, stamp and etch. Lets get started!

"Whether it is making art, composing music or designing a garden, I believe that each of us is her best self when creating."

Heather Thomas

Stash Buster
weaving fabric

Weaving fabric strips is one of the oldest ways to manipulate fabric. Any basket-weaving pattern can be used, although some patterns will take more time and imagination.

*Techniques: **Curved Weaving**; Hand Embroidery; Machine Lace Appliqué*

basic weaving

Most of us remember weaving strips of construction paper as children; if the pattern is very detailed in color and design it is a good idea to first make a paper mock-up to have a reference piece. The pattern and color combinations are endless so let yourself go. For the purpose of this exercise the warp strips refer to vertical strips and the weft refers to the horizontal strips.

supplies

- Two 12-inch fabric squares
- Light-weight spray starch
- Foam board
- Long flat flower-head pins
- Lightweight fusible stabilizer
- Stiletto or pencil with eraser

1 Fold one piece of fabric and draw a line about 1 inch from the open edge opposite the fold. From the fold, make straight cuts up to the drawn line, measuring a ¾-inch space between cuts.

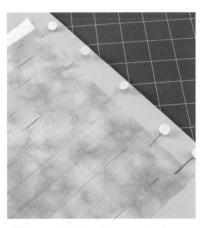

2 Unfold the fabric and place it flat and right-side down on the foam board—this will serve as the warp. Pin the fabric to the board at the uncut edges. Be sure your fabric is wrong side up.

3 For the weft, cut twelve ¾-inch-wide strips from the second piece of fabric. Weave a weft strip, right-side down, over and under the warp strips, snug it up with the stiletto or pencil eraser, and pin. Repeat until all the strips are used.

4 Make sure there is no space between warp and weft. Cut a piece of stabilizer the size of your work and press, fusible side down, onto the weaving. Do not rub your iron back and forth or it will move the pattern out of alignment. Let cool and turn over.

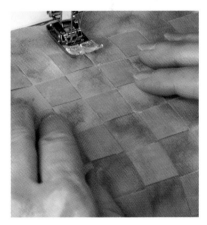

5 Stitch along the warp and weft edges until they are all stitched down in both directions. There are many ways to stitch the raw edges of the strips. The most common is a straight stitch on either side of the warp and weft, or a narrow satin stitch.

curved weaving

Adding a little playful movement to your weaving is easily done by cutting your strips in a wavy manner. For complex weaving, cut each strip from a different fabric to make a multi-color base fabric for your page.

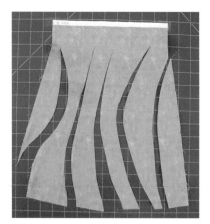

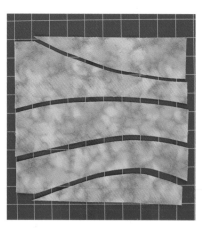

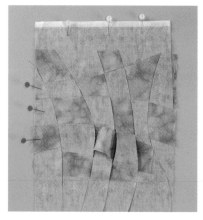

1 Using the rotary cutter, randomly cut curved strips for the warp from one fabric, stopping just 1 inch from the edge. From another fabric cut curved strips for the weft. (Here, the fabrics were right side up when cut, so before weaving they need to be turned right side down to allow for the interfacing.) Vary the curves so you have a narrow center and wide ends or a wide center with narrow ends—just play around with your orphan or stash fabrics.

2 Turn the strips right-side down. Weave the strips as described on the previous page, being sure to adjust with your stiletto or pencil eraser and pinning them at the edges. Follow Steps 4 and 5 on the previous page to finish your woven fabric.

3 For even more variety, use a different color or kind of fabric for each strip, just be sure to not get the pieces out of order and remember to work right-side down so you can apply fusible interfacing after weaving. Work as follows: Cut the most left warp strip. Lap the right edge of this first strip of fabric over the second strip. Cut the second strip using the right edge of the first strip as a cutting guide. Pin the first strip to the foam board. Use the second strip as a guide for the third strip, pinning each strip to the board as you go. Cut the weft strips, starting at the top, using the same method.

 tips

- Press and starch fabric before cutting.

- Keep the fabric pieces in the order they were cut (especially the curved pieces).

- Take extra time to snug the pieces up to each other.

- Mark straight lines on the foam board as a guide to keep edges straight.

- Don't want to stitch down all those strip edges? Iron Steam-a-Seam2 to the back of your fabrics before cutting strips. Cut the strips, peel the paper and weave. With a Teflon pad underneath, press the woven piece, effectively fusing together the overlapping strip sections. Keep in mind this method is not washable.

- Try different weaving patterns and decorative machine stitches.

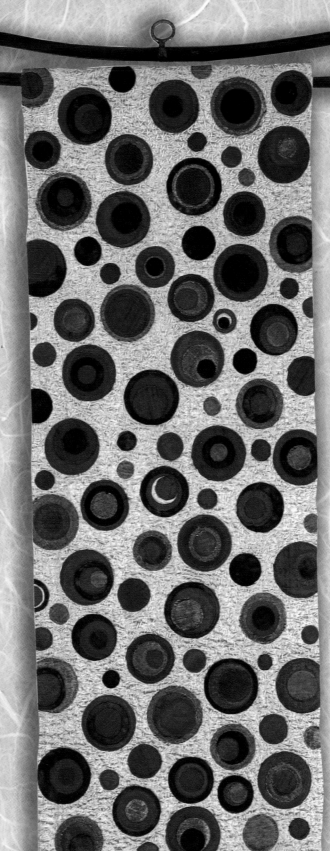

Circles #3
11 x 31 inches
Ruth Chandler

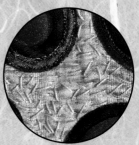

Ricing

Going for Texture
tic-tac-toe tucks

Tucks create texture, depth and interest rarely found in commercial fabrics. The effect may look intricate but the technique is actually quite simple and works up fast. Plus, it's lots of fun!

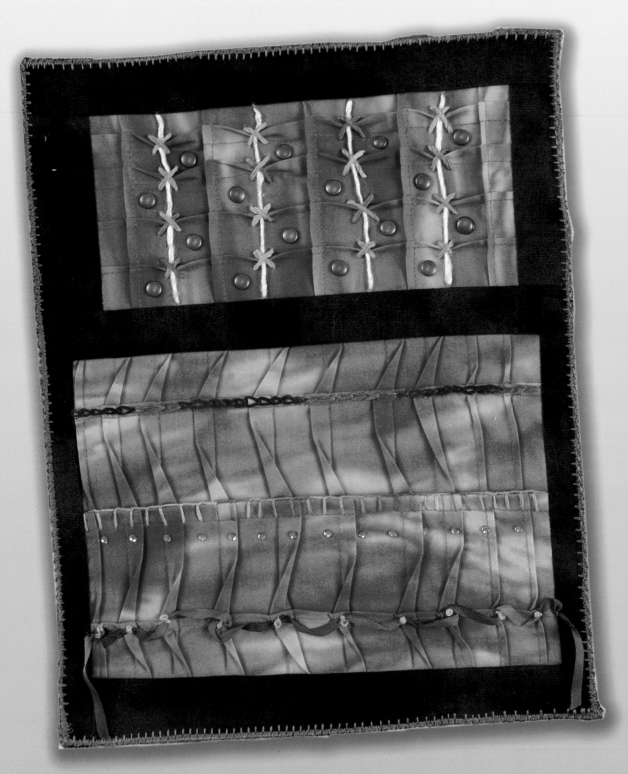

*Techniques: **Tucks**, Embroidery, Iron-on Metal Dots*

tic-tac-toe tucks

Before gathering trims, paints and assorted appliques, let's first discover how you can embellish your project by just working with the fabric itself. Playing with fabric is a great way to reduce your stash or use up those prints you once thought were so fabulous but were not once you got them home. Try some tucks in a variety of ways and be amazed at the effects they can create.

supplies: fabric, thread, spray starch

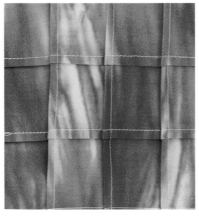

1 Fold a piece of lightly starched fabric widthwise, right side out, and press the fold. Sew a straight seam, ¼ to ½ inch from the pressed fold. Evenly divided, repeat three times, for a total of four tucks across the fabric. Press the tucks in either direction, all the same or opposite.

2 Next, stitch four or more vertical tucks in the same manner. The fabric now resembles a tic-tac-toe grid. For variety, try using the same depth of tucks sewn in both directions but vary the width and angle.

 tips

- One of the easiest ways to add texture to fabric is to fold and stitch. There are several ways to describe this technique but the most common term is pin-tucks. Pin-tucks bring to mind old-fashioned blouses or dresses, but this is a contemporary take.

- Although tucks are traditionally measured with equal depth and width, this method allows for more freedom and no measuring. Start with a pressed and lightly starched piece of fabric roughly twice the size of the desired finished piece—this is generous and can be smaller depending on the width and depth of the tucks.

- For the purpose of this section two terms are used to describe the tuck: 'depth' refers to the amount of fabric folded over and 'width' refers to the space between each tuck. If the depth is much more than ½ inch it loses the tuck look and becomes a bulky pleat.

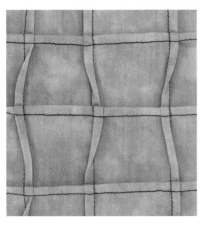

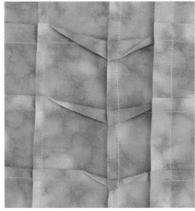

3 Here's another option: Before stitching the vertical tucks, create some movement by pressing sections of the horizontal tucks in a different direction.

4 Another technique to try is to vary the depth of each tuck in both vertical as well as horizontal directions.

Adding Flair
stitches & bits

Embellishing does not get any easier than this! Augment your tucks with leftover trims of all kinds and a variety of threads to create a whole new fabric.

*Techniques: **Stitches and Bits,** Tucks*

adding stitches and bits to tucks

Stitching bits of fiber into the tucks gives a whole new look and feel to these tucks. In order to hold down the extra bulk, this technique is slightly different from the previous one. Sewing decorative machine stitches on the tuck edges adds yet another creative touch.

supplies: fabric, thread, various trims, ribbons and fabric strips

1 Fold and press the fabric as you would for the tuck but do not stitch the tuck. Open up the tuck and insert the trim underneath the fold; close the tuck. Stitch the tuck as close to the folded edge as possible. Because of the bulky nature this technique is best used in only one direction; however, stitching at an angle can add a lot of interest.

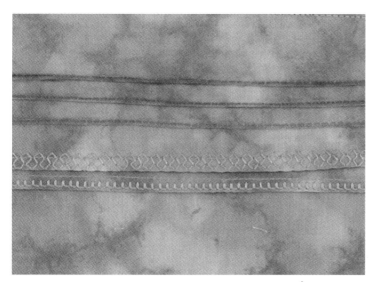

2 By using a programmed machine stitch, instead of a straight stitch, you can add a lot of variety to your tucks. Pay attention to the width of the stitch and keep in mind that these stitches will add bulk, so this option is best sewn in only one direction. Also try it at a 45- or 60-degree angle.

tips

- Press fabrics.

- For additional crispness use light starch, such as Best Press.

- Use solid, tone-on-tone or very small print fabric.

- Vary thread color for design.

FIBERS TO TRY:

- Lace—Try different weights but avoid thick edges.

- Rick Rack—Experiment with all widths, from very narrow to very wide.

- Ribbon—Use velvet, organza, gross-grain and hand dyes but avoid thick and wired ribbons.

- Fabric—Fold narrow strips of fabric and tuck the raw edges under the fold or leave the raw edges exposed.

- Piping—Tuck piping into the fold, making sure the piping's seam allowances disappear completely into the fold.

- Yarns—Choose lightweight novelty yarns such as eyelash or the ones that look like fringe.

- Gathers and Pleats—Gather or pleat ribbons or fabric before sliding them underneath the tuck.

Another Dimension
bubbles & wrinkles

Add dimension to your fabric by poking it into the holes of a grid and
letting it dry—creating big bold bubbles. Wrinkling is a quick, easy technique that
adds texture and interest to fabric and you can't do it wrong!

*Techniques: **Bubbles & Wrinkles**, Machine Embroidery, Iron-on Crystals, Wool Beads*

bubbling

Any grid with uniform openings can be used; however, openings larger than one inch will not hold the fabric long enough to dry and grids smaller than ⅛ inch are just too small. Kitchen-supply and hardware stores are great places to find interesting grids—a raised cooling rack works well. Use any fabric that will not shrink much and, a good rule of thumb is, the thicker the fabric, the larger the openings in the grid. When playing with different fabrics, such as organza or silk taffeta, try not to use water as some fabrics have a tendency to spot.

supplies

- Fabric—twice the size of the desired finished piece
- Gridded appliance such as cooling rack or metal basket
- Fusible interfacing
- Chopstick or pencil

1 Thoroughly wet the fabric and squeeze out the excess water. Raise the grid at least ½ inch above your work surface to allow enough space underneath for the fabric bubbles. Loosely place the fabric, right side down, onto the grid. Beginning in the center and using the large end of a chopstick, or the eraser end of a pencil, gently poke the fabric into the grid openings.

2 The fabric will have a tendency to pull out so keep the fabric loose and hold down the already poked sections. Use a spray bottle to keep the fabric damp. Continue pushing the fabric through the grid until enough holes are filled for your purpose. Allow the fabric to dry completely.

3 Before popping the bubbles out of the grid openings, cut a piece of fusible interfacing and press, fusible side down, onto the back of the gridded fabric. Remove fabric from grid.

4 You can secure the bubbles by stitching between the bubbles as they have a tendency to pull loose. Try adding glass beads or French knots, or couch fibers around the bubbles.

5 For smaller bubbles, work with a smaller grid. Here, a basket from the office-supply store created a very densely bubbled surface.

wrinkling

Wrinkling is yet another technique to reduce your stash of undesirable fabric. After wrinkling, your workable fabric will be quite a bit smaller so a good rule of thumb is to begin with double the desired finished size. Use your wrinkled fabric as is or stitch down a few wrinkles with decorative threads.

supplies: fabric—twice the size of the desired finished piece, old panty hose, fusible interfacing

1 The best way for fabric to hold wrinkles, folds, or pleats, is to get it completely wet and dry-in the wrinkles. To get started, wet the fabric and then twist it into a rope. If desired, you can first roughly finger-pleat the fabric before twisting.

2 Keep twisting your fabric until the rope begins to twist on itself. Continue twisting until the rope curls up into a ball. Scrunch the ball some more until it's very tight.

3 Stuff the ball into the leg of an old pair of panty hose. Tie a knot in the leg and snug it up to the ball. To dry, hang up the leg 24–48 hours until the fabric is dry or put it in the dryer with several towels. Remove the dry fabric ball from the panty hose by cutting off the knot and gently undo the ball, leaving the wrinkles.

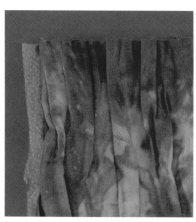

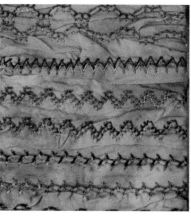

tips

- Stitch a variety of fibers onto the wrinkled surface.
- Attach beads along or on top of random wrinkles.
- Use the wrinkled piece in a quilt block or use as a garment pocket or accent.

4 Place the fabric, wrong-side up, on an ironing board, leaving as many or as few wrinkles as desired. Cut a piece of fusible interfacing to your desired size and press the fusible side to the wrong side of the fabric.

5 Using a straight or narrow satin stitch, randomly stitch down the wrinkles. This is a great opportunity to use some of the decorative stitches that may be pre-programmed in your machine.

There was a little girl,
Who had a little curl,
Right in the middle of her forehead.
When she was good,
She was very good indeed,
But when she was bad she was horrid.

Betty Jane
17½ x 17½ inches
Liz Kettle

Thread Lace Appliqué
Printing on Fabric
Couching
Stamping
Beading
Sequins

Crazy Quilting traditional style

Irregular piecing, ornate embellishments and handstitching are the hallmarks of classic crazy quilting. Contemporary piecing techniques and tools make the traditional style easy to achieve.

Techniques: ***Crazy Quilting***, *Hand Embroidery, Machine Embroidery, Couching, Charms*

traditional style

Mixing a variety of fabrics is essential to crazy quilting—traditionally, wool, velvet, scraps of old clothing and linens are combined with cottons. Assembling the block means simply covering a piece of muslin with randomly cut strips of fabric around a central focus piece. For an interesting composition, cut the strips in differing widths and randomly tilt them as they are added.

supplies: 7-inch square of high thread-count muslin, variety of fabric scraps cut into 1- to 2-inch-wide strips, irregular five-sided shape cut from a 2-inch square of focal fabric

1 Place the focal fabric slightly off-center on top of the muslin square. A quality muslin with a high thread count is preferred to hold up to the multiple seams.

2 Select a narrow fabric strip and, with right sides together, sew with an ⅛-inch seam and very short stitches to the focal fabric. Each strip should be longer than the edge to which it is sewn.

3 Flip the strip right side up and press; do *not* trim.

4 Select another narrow strip and stitch to the next edge of the focal piece in the same manner, making sure to stitch across the first strip. Trim the tail end of the first strip, being careful not to cut the muslin.

5 Flip the second strip right side up and press. Trim the tail end of each fabric strip after attaching the next strip. You may need to remove a few stitches to accomplish the trimming.

6 Using wider strips as you work toward the outer edges of the muslin square, add more strips, until the muslin square is completely covered. Trim your work to a 6½-inch square.

Crazy Quilting deconstructed

Deconstructed crazy quilting borrows signature elements from traditional crazy quilting, blows them apart and reassembles them in a fresh and funky manner.

Techniques: **Deconstructed Crazy Quilting**, *Embroidery, Couching, Printing on Ribbon, Beading*

deconstructed

During the deconstructed machine-stitching process, the edges of the block take on an organic and slightly irregular appearance. Rough edges, fraying, and the occasional wild thread add to the charm of deconstructed crazy quilting so trimming the block to a specific size is not necessary.

supplies: 7-inch square of lightweight fusible stabilizer, variety of fabric scraps, variety of decorative threads including rayon and metallic

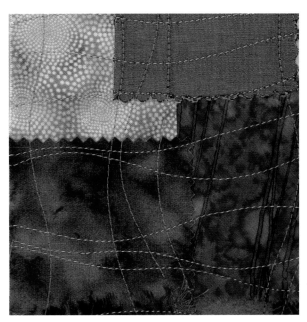

1 Randomly place fabric pieces, right side up, on the fusible side of the stabilizer. Move the fabrics around until the composition is attractive, making sure the fabrics overlap and no stabilizer shows from the right side; pin in place. Turn to the wrong side and fuse the stabilizer to the fabric pieces.

2 Turn right side up and remove the pins. Select a 30wt. rayon thread in a color that coordinates with most the fabric pieces. Using the regular straight stitch setting on your machine, sew horizontal and vertical wavy lines to secure the overlapping fabric pieces to the stabilizer.

3 Using programmed stitches, further embellish the fabric, changing the thread color and/or thread type each time you change the stitch. A large zigzag stitch can act as an embellishment guide. If you have an advanced machine, embroidery patterns such as flowers and leaves have wonderful potential as a background for future bead work.

 tips

- An important characteristic of the look comes from the use of many different types of fabrics. Combine different fabric types with cottons for a rich, complex look.

- Don't be afraid to cut the edges of the fabric pieces with pinking shears or, at times, leave some raw edges to enhance variety. Selvages can provide a wonderful, unexpected effect.

Add a Personal Touch
rubber stamping

Crafts and hobby stores sell an abundance of ready made stamps
for paper crafters, interior designers and fabric artists. Master this simple
stamping technique and transform the ordinary into extra-ordinary.

Techniques: ***Rubber Stamping,*** *Beading*

rubber stamping

Before you begin playing with your stamps and paints, cover your work table with plastic and tape it down. Iron the pre-washed fabric and tape it on the plastic-covered table. Choose a color palette and mix all the paint colors you plan on using. Practice stamping on paper before jumping in on the fabric.

supplies

- Fabric paints in a variety of colors or acrylic paints with fabric medium added

- Stamps—rubber, foam, wood or metal—in a variety of shapes, styles and sizes

- Foam brushes or rollers, 1–3 inches in width

- Scrap paper or paper towel

- Paint containers, mixing sticks, masking tape, cup for water, measuring spoon

- Pre-washed fabric: choose solids or near solids—batiks work great

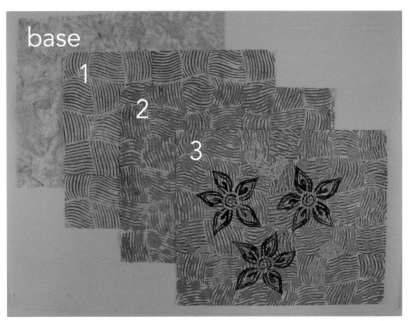

base
1
2
3

1 Decide how many design layers you plan to add to the surface of your fabric. Three is a good number but you can add as few as one or as many as you want. Just remember, the more paint you add the stiffer your fabric becomes.

Each stamped design layer should be different in both size and style of motif. This example uses three layers and four stamps.

For the first layer, consider a textural design and a color similar to your base fabric. For the second layer change the textural design and add a new color. For the final layer choose a design motif such as a leaf or flower and a color that coordinates yet contrasts with the previous colors.

 tips

- Use a color wheel to help mix custom colors.

- To make a paint color lighter begin with white then add in the colored paint until you have reached the depth of color you desire.

- To make a paint color darker, begin with the color and add small drops of black until you reach the desired shade.

- To make a paint color less intense, to tone it down, begin with the color and add either gray or brown in small drops until you reach the desired tone.

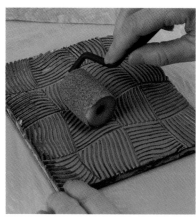

1   Pick up the stamp for the first layer and dab the wide, flat side of the brush into the paint until saturated. Do not overload the brush or the stamp with paint. Tap the brush on a paper towel to eliminate excess paint. Tap the flat, wide side of the foam brush onto the stamp rather than brushing it on. Do not overload the brush or the stamp with paint.

2   If you are using a roller, roll it into the paint until saturated, then roll on a paper towel to eliminate excess paint. Roll an even layer of paint across the stamp's surface. When the stamp is completely covered with paint, check to make sure there are no areas where the paint is too thick and globby—remove excess with a dry roller, or too thin—apply more.

3   Hold the stamp, paint side down, in both hands, about 1 inch above the area you wish to stamp. Carefully lower the stamp onto the fabric and then, with your hands flat, press down with even, but not hard, pressure. Lift off the stamp. Repeat until the entire surface is covered; let dry. Using your other stamps, apply the next layer, then the next, etc. until your fabric is finished.

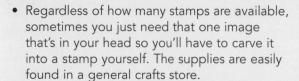

tips

- Regardless of how many stamps are available, sometimes you just need that one image that's in your head so you'll have to carve it into a stamp yourself. The supplies are easily found in a general crafts store.

- Use the Speedy Cut or Mastercarve block in the size it was made or cut it into smaller sections for several smaller stamps. Be sure to leave at least 1 inch of 'free' space around your design so you have something to hold on to.

- Carving can be done freestyle, or draw or transfer a design on the block before carving. Use a pencil to draw directly on the block or draw with a pencil on paper, using a heavy line, then turn the paper over onto the block and burnish the drawing onto the block with the edge of a coin.

- If you want to carve words or letters into the block you must use the burnishing method so the word will be backwards on the stamp to enable it to print properly on the fabric.

100 Years of Solitude
36 x 42 inches
Heather Thomas

Dimensional Appliqué

Rubber Stamping

Peek-a-Boo
fashion a frame

A frame highlights a special embellishment or creates a focal element. This technique can be used in most quilts and with most any embellishment and is delightfully effective for accentuating photo transfers or prints from your computer.

*Techniques: **Fashion a Frame**, Stamping, Ricing, Mini Marbles, Printing on Ribbon*

making a frame

When making a frame, the cut-out area is faced with a matching fabric to neatly finish the edges of the opening. Here, a square opening is cut to highlight a fabric stamped with script and a dragonfly. Try a triangle, circle, or organic shape to emphasize your focal element.

supplies: 6½-inch fabric square or small quilt block, 4-inch fabric square for the facing, marking pencil, small piece of fabric with an interesting image or embellishment to fit your desired opening

1 Determine the location and size for the frame. On the wrong side of the facing fabric, draw a frame outline. With right sides together, center the facing fabric on the fabric or quilt block. Sew on top of the outline, making sure to lock the stitches.

2 Draw a second outline *inside* the stitched outline and ¼ inch from the stitches. Cutting on this second outline, cut away both layers—the fabric or quilt block and the facing fabric—inside the stitched outline, revealing a frame.

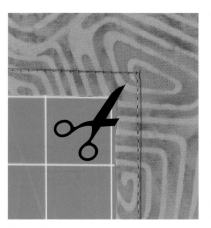

3 Clip the seam allowance to the corners of the opening. Fold the facing fabric through the frame to the wrong side of the fabric or quilt block.

4 The facing fabric is now on the wrong side of your work and the seam allowances are hidden. Press for a crisp frame opening.

5 Place fabric with imagery or embellishment behind the opening and topstitch in place on the right side, ⅛ inch outside the frame edges.

Images on Fabric
inkjet printing

Whether you use commercially prepared fabric sheets or fabric you prep yourself,
adding images to fabric is a favorite technique for personalizing your work.
For unique results, play with different fabrics—silk, canvas, cotton.

*Techniques: **Inkjet Printing (commercial fabric)**, Printing on Ribbon, Wool Beads*

commercial inkjet fabric

Use your digital photos or scan personal photos, drawings or even fresh flowers into your computer to print custom fabric. You can find a variety of commercial inkjet fabric sheets in the fabric store and online. Get together with a group of friends to purchase several brands and find out which one best suits your purpose. Depending on the size of the photo, drawing or object, be sure to print multiples on one sheet of fabric to be cost effective.

supplies

- Computer and inkjet printer
- Scanner (optional)
- Image or text you want to print on fabric
- Commercial inkjet fabric sheets

1 Prepare your image for printing in your photo editing software. Every printer is different so try different settings to achieve the results you want. If possible, start by setting your software to 'best' photo and matte paper. Keep a written record of different settings for future reference.

2 Place the fabric sheet in the paper tray of your printer, referring to your printer manual for proper orientation as some printers feed face up and some feed face down. If you're not sure, place a mark on a regular sheet of paper and run it through the printer to find out where your mark is positioned after printing. Print your image. If your printer has any difficulty grabbing the paper, gently guide the fabric into the printer as it starts to feed. Allow the image to dry thoroughly before removing the fabric from the carrier. Set the image with a hot iron and use as desired.

- The type of ink in your printer makes a difference in the longevity of your printed fabric image:
- Pigment inks— are more water and fade resistant than dye inks and are generally more expensive.
- Dye inks— usually produce sharper images and more vibrant colors. When using a dye ink, pre-treat your fabric with a solution such as Bubble Jet Set 2000, InkAid or matte Golden's Digital Ground.
- Both inks will print on fabric without problems but care needs to be taken against fading.

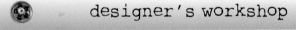
designer's workshop

Using different kinds of inkjet fabric sheets can be a fun and interesting way to make your project unique.

making your own printing sheets

Keeping down cost is just one reason for making your own fabric printing sheets. The best reason, though, is that you can use any fabric you like, be it solid or printed, cotton or silk. As long as your printer will transport the fabric, any fabric is game for your creative urges.

supplies

* Washed and ironed fabric (try cotton, PFD muslin, silk, organza or canvas)

• Freezer paper or Avery full sheet clear inkjet labels

• Rotary cutter, ruler and mat

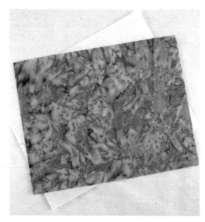

FREEZER PAPER

1 Cut the freezer paper to the size of your printer paper. Cut the fabric slightly larger than the freezer paper. Place the freezer paper, shiny side up, on your ironing surface. Place your fabric, right side up, on the freezer paper.

2 Press well with a hot iron to form a temporary bond between the paper and the fabric, making sure there are no bubbles or ripples. After pressing, trim your fabric to the exact size of the freezer paper.

To print, run your fabric/freezer paper sheet through the printer as you would a regular paper sheet.

CLEAR INKJET LABEL

1 Cut fabric slightly larger than the label and place right side down on your workspace. Place the label on the fabric with the backing face-down.

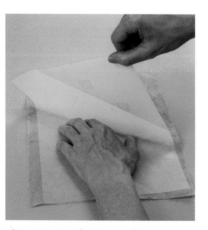

2 Begin peeling a corner from the label's backing sheet. Place the exposed label corner on a corner of the fabric, sticky side to the back of the fabric, and slowly pull back the label backing while you smooth label and fabric together, making sure you don't have any bubbles or ripples.

3 If desired, you can smooth the label onto the fabric using a ruler. Trim the fabric to the size of the label sheet.

To print, run your fabric/clear label sheet through the printer as you would a regular sheet of paper.

Adding Text
printing on ribbon

Many fabric pages in this book feature hand-dyed ribbon accents with printed text indicating which techniques are used. Ribbon choices are unlimited so try a few different kinds to see what works best for your project.
Find fun fonts online or check out some of the scrapbooking font disks.

supplies

- Computer and inkjet printer
- Rayon, silk or cotton ribbon
- Paper
- Double sided tape

1 In your word processing program type your desired text, leaving enough spacing between free-standing words so you can cut the ribbon between them. Space the lines to allow for the ribbon width. Print the text on a sheet of printer paper. Do not close the program.

2 Apply double sided tape directly on top of the printed words. The tape can be slightly narrower than your ribbon. If your ribbon is very wide you can use two strips of tape to secure the ribbon to the paper, keeping in mind that all the tape should be covered with ribbon.

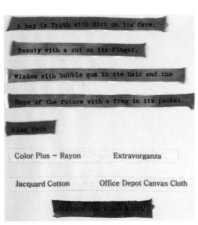

tips

- To prevent fraying, paint the cut ribbon ends with clear nail polish.
- Polyester and nylon ribbon can be used but the ink may bleed slightly.

3 Smooth the ribbon onto the tape, taking care not to stretch the ribbon. The double sided tape should be completely covered by the ribbon so it will not stick to the printer rollers. The first two strips of ribbon on this example need to be longer.

4 Place the paper with ribbon into your printer and print again. Allow some time for the ink to dry and then carefully peel the ribbon off the tape.

Inked Inspiration
photo transfer

If printing directly on fabric does not trip your trigger try your hand at transferring an image to fabric. The transfer can be accomplished in several ways—here, we use transparency film from the office supply store and a commercial transfer paper.

Techniques: ***Transparency Film Transfer,*** *Embossed Metal, Found Objects*

transparency film transfer

Print your images to transparency film using an ink jet printer. If you are printing text be sure to activate the 'mirror image' or 'reverse image' option. Put as many images, quotes, etc. as possible on each sheet of transparency film as it is quite pricey and one sheet can get you several transfers. Here, we coat the printed transparency with rubbing alcohol and then transfer the image—for a different effect, try applying the rubbing alcohol to the fabric and then burnishing the image onto the fabric.

supplies

- Inkjet transparency film (not quick-dry) or Transfer Artist Paper
- Inkjet printer
- Fabric to receive the image
- Rubbing alcohol
- Fine mist spray bottle or plant mister

1 Choose the transparency or plain paper setting on the print menu. You may have to experiment to find your ideal setting. If needed, consult your printer manual. Transparency film has a right and wrong side. Check your specific brand for printing instructions. Generally, the side to print on is slightly rough. Print your image on the transparency film. Allow the image to dry.

2 Trim the image from the transparency sheet, leaving a large enough margin to grasp. Pour some rubbing alcohol into the spray bottle. Be sure to mark this bottle so it cannot be confused with water. Iron your fabric and place on a smooth, clean, hard surface. Liberally spray the ink side of the transparency image with the rubbing alcohol.

3 Carefully place the image, ink side down, onto the receiving fabric.

4 Burnish the image by rubbing in a circular motion with the back of a wooden spoon or scissors handle, applying firm, but not hard, pressure.

5 Lift one corner of the transparency and slowly peel it back, checking to see if the image has properly transferred. If the image has not transferred sufficiently, lay the film back down and continue to rub. Keep in mind that the image will not transfer perfectly. Fabrics with images transferred in this manner are not washable.
NOTE: This product is used in a manner for which it is not intended and changes in the products may affect the success of transfers. Experiment and record your results.

transfer artist paper

If you need to be able to wash the fabric that has your transfer, then Transfer Artist Paper is your answer. For those who don't have an inkjet printer, draw or make a design with crayons, markers or colored pencils on this special paper and then transfer to your fabric.

1 Choose the plain paper setting in the print menu. If you are printing text be sure to activate the mirror image or reverse image setting option. The printing surface of Transfer Artist Paper is white, the back is blue. Print the image on the Transfer Artist Paper. Allow the image to dry. Trim the printed image close to the image edges.

2 Iron your fabric and place on a smooth, clean surface. Place the image, ink side down, onto the receiving fabric and press with a hot iron for 6–10 seconds. Do not slide the iron; press down only. Irons with many steam holes or dimples will leave some areas un-transferred. Repress those areas with the smooth part of your iron's sole plate.

3 Carefully lift one corner of the backing paper off the fabric and slowly pull it back. If the image has not transferred completely place the backing paper down again and press with the hot iron. Fabrics with images transferred with Transfer Artist Paper are washable.

 designer's workshop

In each printing and transferring exercise Liz used the same photo of her grandson Kristopher on purpose—and, no, it's not just because he is the apple of her eye!

Using the same photo gives you an excellent tool for comparison of the various printing and transfer media and their effects on the fabric.

Blessings
10 x 26 inches
Liz Kettle

Images on Fabric
Beading
Hand Embroidery
Couching

Magical Medium
printing on lutradur

Lutradur can be painted or printed on, stitched, stamped, cut and melted. No wonder it is so popular! Here, fresh flowers are scanned and printed on this magical medium; then cut out.

Techniques: **Printing on Lutradur,** *Tucks, Hand Embroidery*

lutradur

Lutradur is a nonwoven stabilizer with properties of both paper and fabric. It is lightweight, translucent and fairly stiff and is available in 70wt. and a slightly heavier 100wt. When printing on Lutradur, use an Avery full-sheet label as carrier to support the Lutradur through the printer.

supplies

- 8½ x 11-inch piece of 70wt. Lutradur

- Scan of fresh flowers or photograph

- Clear gesso or matte medium

- Foam brush

- Scissors or heat tool

1 Using a foam brush paint a thin layer of clear gesso or matte medium on the Lutradur and let dry. Capture fresh flowers with your scanner or prepare your chosen image for printing. Print the image on the gessoed side of the Lutradur.

2 Using scissors or a heat tool, cut the flower images from the Lutradur. The heat tool allows for easy cutting of spaces at the base of the petals and yields an organic edge rather than the crisp edge obtained with scissors. When using a heat tool to cut Lutradur, place the Lutradur on a flat metal surface such as the back of a cookie sheet.

3 For the lattice background, cut a 20 x 32-inch piece of fabric. Referring to the directions on page 19 for a tic-tac-toe tucked grid, make a grid of tucks using ¼-inch tucks spaced 1 inch apart. To create the lattice-look cut the gridded fabric at a 45-degree angle.

Distribute the Lutradur flowers on your lattice fabric and attach them with French knots in the center of each flower, stitching through all the layers.

Fun & Easy discharge dyeing

A fun and easy-to-master technique for creating one of a kind fabrics, discharge dyeing is the practice of taking away, or discharging, color. Choose from three different discharge products—each product has its advantages and disadvantages.

Techniques: **Discharge Dyeing Gel Bleach**, *Couching, Beading*

gel bleach pen

The gel bleach in the pen has a mixed consistency. Though a gel, it seems to separate from the bleach and both come out at one time, gel surrounded by liquid bleach (shaking to mix helps, but one can not shake constantly). The pen's opening is somewhat large so a fine line is not attainable (lines end up about 1/4 inch wide). Because of the constant shaking, bubbles are formed that come out of the tip, causing a dappled effect on the fabric. Therefore, this product, though easy to use, can be a little hard to control. The product can be squeezed into a small container and used for stenciling or stamping. It has a light, bleachy smell.

supplies

- Gel Bleach Pen or Dishwasher Gel with Bleach

- Soft Scrub with Bleach (do not use a store brand as it is not consistent)

- Jaquard Discharge Paste

- Solid natural fabric or slightly mottled batik (check to make sure each fabric will discharge by placing a drop of discharge product on a corner of the fabric; wait five minutes then rinse.)

- Squeeze bottle with fine tip (not needed if using Gel Bleach Pen)

- 1- or 2-inch foam brush and small container

- Rubber or foam stamps, nylon net or other resist material such as plastic stencil or metal screening

- Anti-Chlor tablets (not if using Discharge Paste)

- Rubber gloves

1 Use either a bleach pen, as shown here, or fill a fine tipped squeeze bottle with Soft Scrub or Discharge Paste. If the opening to your squeeze bottle is very small, fill a plastic bag with the discharge product, cut off a corner, place the cut corner into the opening of the bottle and squeeze the product into the bottle. Draw your design on the fabric using a chalk pencil or just free-hand-draw directly from the pen.

2 Allow the gel to dry completely. Rinse, soak five minutes in an Anti-Chlor bath, then launder.

tips

- All discharge products should be used in a well ventilated area.

- Cover work surfaces in plastic and wear old clothes. Plastic gloves are optional.

- Fabrics with Soft Scrub or Gel Bleach Pen should be allowed to dry, then rinsed out thoroughly with warm water; next, soaked for five minutes in a bath of Anti-Chlor (follow manufacturer's direction for mixing in water), then laundered.

- Fabrics with Discharge Paste should be allowed to dry thoroughly, then heated with a steam iron to activate, then laundered.

soft scrub

Soft Scrub has a thick, grainy, consistency and is easy to use with stencils or any other type of resist and a foam brush. You can get a relatively fine line when extruded through a fine-tipped bottle and it does not bubble. Soft Scrub dries quickly and is available in fragranced options, which lessens the often overwhelming bleach smell. Its downfall is that it dries up in the container between uses and has to be stirred or shaken often.

1 Decant some Soft Scrub into a small fine-tipped bottle. When writing on fabric with the scrub, it is easier to just free-hand your words, rather than trace pre-written words. Have some throw-away fabric on hand to practice on before you commit your good fabric to this treatment.

2 Place your fabric on a plastic covered table and top with the net; tape both layers in place. Pour a small amount of Soft Scrub into a bowl. Dip a foam brush into the product and lightly tap onto the mesh. Don't overload your brush—you don't want to lose the definition of your resist.

3 Allow the Soft Scrub to dry completely. Next, rinse, soak five minutes in an Anti-Chlor bath, and then launder.

discharge paste

Though this product is called 'paste' it is thick and gelatinous. It has a somewhat strange smell and is less caustic than bleach. Very easy to control, you can squeeze it through a small-tipped bottle or use with resists but it really shines when used with rubber stamps. Once applied, let dry completely; then steam to activate and, finally, wash it out. As suggested for all these products, read the manufacturer's instructions prior to using.

1 Pour the Discharge Paste into a small container and tape your fabric to a plastic covered surface. Using a foam brush, tap the paste onto a rubber stamp.

2 Position the stamp over the the fabric, lower it down, then press in place. Apply more paste and continue stamping until the surface is fully covered with the design.

3 Allow the product to dry completely, then rinse. Steam-iron as directed and, lastly, launder.

Hot! Hot! Hot!
28 x 38 inches
Heather Thomas

Couching

Instant Age rusting fabric

Try this technique to add instant age to your fabric. Using standard hardware, a splash of vinegar and some muslin, you can create this overnight transformation.

rusting

beading

decorative brads

*Techniques: **Rusting Fabric**, Beading, Sequins, Decorative Brads*

rusting fabric

Before you pile on the washers, pins and other hardware pieces be sure your fabric is PFD—Prepared For Dyeing, which means pre-washed and dried without using fabric softener.

supplies: PFD fabric, small hardware pieces such as T-pins, washers, screws, etc., white vinegar, spray bottle

 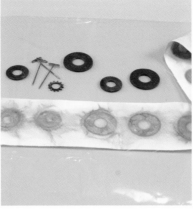

1 Cover your work surface with plastic. Mix equal parts water and vinegar in a spray bottle. Lay a piece of PFD (prepared for dye) fabric on the plastic (shown above is a test piece). Spray the fabric with an equal vinegar/water mixture until saturated. Arrange hardware such as washers, T-pins and screws on one half of the saturated fabric. Fold the other half of the fabric over the half with the hardware. Make sure the fabric is sopping wet with the vinegar and water mixture; if needed, spray some more. Cover everything with a second piece of plastic.

2 Depending on how 'rusty' you want the fabric, leave it under the plastic for 24 hours to a full week; just make sure it stays wet. Check the fabric every once in a while. When the rust level is to your satisfaction, open the plastic and carefully remove the rusty pieces of hardware. Use care especially with the pins. Rinse the fabric for several minutes under running water to remove excess rust and vinegar. There may be heavy odor. If so, you can run the fabric through a machine wash cycle, but this may take away too much of the rust. Iron the fabric and cut it up into pieces suitable for a quilt.

tips

- Keep your rusty hardware parts because you can use them again. Another reason to hold on to the rusty hardware: Spray them with a fixative and sew them onto art quilts and other projects as found objects.

- Speed up the rusting process by adding about a tablespoon of bleach to the water and vinegar mixture. Be careful with this technique because it does tend to make the fabric fragile over time. Depending on the look you are going for, this can be a good or a bad thing.

- Large rusted items such as huge pieces of hardware, farm equipment, sculptures, most anything that is rusted (I have an old milk jug with writing embossed on it) are fabulous to use for rusting fabric. Just place a saturated piece of fabric on top of them and keep the fabric wet with the vinegar solution, wrap plastic over the fabric if you can, otherwise, just keep spraying it with the solution until you like the amount of rust transferred to the fabric. Also, wrapping and scrunching fabric around an old, rusty coffee can will produce a shibori effect.

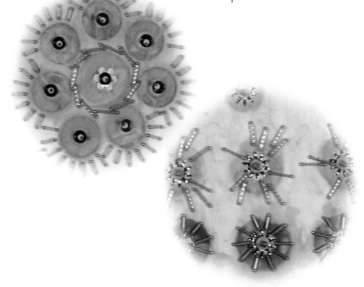

Etch Away
dévoré or burn-out

Dévoré is a fancy word for etching away fabric, using caustic chemicals that 'devour' natural fibers. The effects of dévoré can be very different depending on which fabric you use.

Techniques: Dévoré, Beading, Machine Embroidery

dévoré

The product used here, Fiber Etch, is based on the chemical Sodium Bisulfate which erodes natural fibers such as cotton and silk but does not affect man made fibers such as polyester and nylon. When applied to a cotton/polyester or silk/polyester blend only the polyester is left behind, the cotton or silk etched away for a 'burn-out' effect. For this exercise, a 100% cotton fabric is used.

supplies

- Fiber Etch by Silkpaint Corporation

- Polyester thread, 50 or 60wt.

- Cotton or other natural fiber fabric or a fabric blend with natural and manmade fibers such as cotton-, rayon-, and silk-polyester blends

- Iron-on tear-away stabilizer such as Totally Stable by Sulky

- Machine Embroidery needle, size 80, 75 or 70

- Blow dryer or heat gun

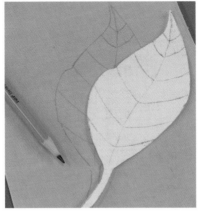

1 Trace or free-hand draw your design to the right side of the fabric with a fine mechanical pencil or with a marking pencil that closely matches the color of thread you're going to use.

2 Iron two layers of stabilizer to the back of the fabric. Load sewing machine with polyester thread and a new embroidery needle and set to zig-zag stitch. Set the stitch width to at least ⅛ inch and the length to the shortest possible. Satin-stitch up the stem and center spine of the leaf, then stitch the veins. Finish by stitching the outline of the leaf. Peel all visible stabilizer from the back of the fabric.

3 Read the manufacturer's instructions for using the Fiber Etch. Open the squeeze bottle and clip the tip of the applicator to make the smallest opening possible. Take caution with the product—

a small drip results in a hole where you may not want a hole so be careful. Place the applicator tip along a satin stitch edge inside the leaf. Lightly squeeze the bottle to extrude a fine line of the product along the edge of the stitching; then use the tip of the bottle to rub it into the fabric. It is not necessary to cover the entire fabric section with product, just make sure you get it right up to the edge of the stitching. Apply Fiber Etch along all the edges of the stitching inside the leaf.

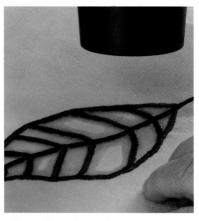

4 Allow the etching liquid to dry or dry with a blow dryer, set on high, or a heat gun, set on low. As the liquid dries the area where it was applied turns dark.

5 Once dry, place the fabric on a protected ironing surface and iron with a medium hot iron just until you see the etched areas turn white or light brown. Be cautious with the iron as overheating will result in a hard black edge next to the stitched line.

6 Using your fingers or an awl, push out the fabric between the stitched lines. Use your finger nail to rub away the fiber right next to the stitched line. Rinse the piece in warm water and a small amount of laundry soap; air dry and iron flat.

7 Place the leaf on the fabric of your choice. Using the same thread you used for the satin stitching and stitching just inside the outer edge of the satin-stitch outline, straight-stitch along the outer edge of the leaf to hold the two layers together.

Tree of Life
18 x 60 inches
Heather Thomas

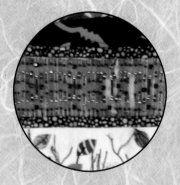

Beading
Dimensional Appliqué
Thread Painting

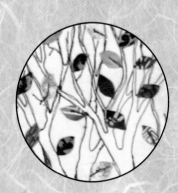

soft embellishments

Soft Embellishing techniques open the door to unlimited possibilities and fun—use one, use them all. Make them flat or dimensional, delicate or chunky, matte or over the top glitzy! Try adding decorative stitches by hand or machine, funky fibers with couching or felting, and a bit of sparkle with foiling, glitter or Angelina fibers. Add thread lace, felting, and Tyvek to your embellishing repertoire. The most difficult part is choosing which one to try first. Many soft embellishments are appropriate for traditional quilts and all of them put your personal mark on home décor, clothing, purses, quilts and mixed media art. Mix them up to create your own unique style.

"When was the last time you gave yourself permission to play?"

Liz Kettle

Pick a Stitch
hand embroidery

Hand-stitched embroidery gives a piece a unique look that would be hard to duplicate by machine. The available fibers range from economical and easy-to-find cotton floss to more expensive silk, hand-dyed, linen, rayon, and wool threads and variegated fibers in many colors.

*Techniques: Hand **Embroidery**, Beading*

hand embroidery

Most important to remember when embroidering by hand is to try and keep the needle on top of the work, making it easier to keep the stitches even. These instructions are for embroidering a quilted piece. To embroider on a single fabric layer, a stabilizer such as Sulky Totally Stable is recommended to prevent the fabric from bunching up and losing its shape. For stitch placement, refer to the diagram on page 61.

supplies: fabric, embroidery floss and threads, embroidery needles, small scissors

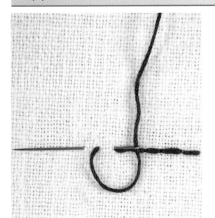

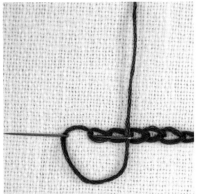

tips

- To begin, bring up the needle from underneath the fabric and bury the knot in the batting.

- Bring the thread down underneath the fabric, knot off and pop the knot into the batting to bury it.

- Floss is hard to detangle; save time and a headache by wrapping it around a small piece of cardboard before you begin.

- Composed of six strands, floss is designed to be separated; vary the amount of strands to create a design element.

- To avoid excessive knotting and tangling, keep thread length to 18–24 inches.

1 BACK STITCH: Keeping the needle on top of the fabric, and working from right to left, come up, go back one stitch length, insert needle and go forward, coming up one stitch length from where thread exits fabric. You are working in a 'two steps forward, one step back' fashion. Repeat until the pattern is finished.

2 CHAIN STITCH: Working on top of the fabric, take a stitch and loop the thread under the needle; pull the thread through. Insert the needle very close to the thread exit; bring back up about ⅛–¼ inch in front of the last stitch. Repeat until design is finished. (To make a detached chain stitch, or Lazy Daisy stitch, secure the loop with a small stitch.)

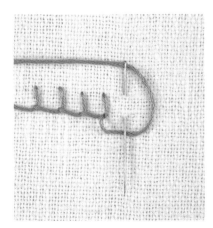

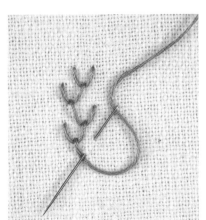

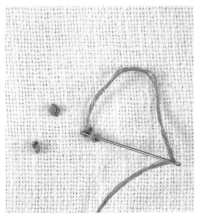

3 BLANKET STITCH: Insert and exit the needle ⅛–¼ inch in front of the first stitch at a right angle. Loop the thread around the point of the needle and pull through. Repeat until the design is completed.

4 FEATHER STITCH: Form a V with the thread and bring the needle down to the bottom of the V. Insert the needle ⅛–¼ inch below the V. The stitches can be in a straight row or can be off-set to create a different pattern. Repeat until finished.

5 FRENCH KNOT: Wrap the thread around the needle about 3–5 times; insert the needle where it exited, keeping the wrapped thread close to the fabric. The more wraps the bigger the knot.

6 RUNNING STITCH: Keeping the needle on top of the fabric, bring the needle in and out of the fabric, making stitches of equal length. The spaces in between the stitches should be of shorter but equal length. Repeat until the pattern is finished.

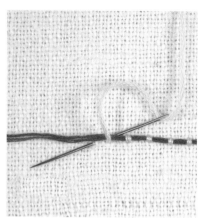

7 COUCHING: Lay down the thread to be couched and, with another thread, tack it down with small stitches worked over the top of the layed-down thread. Repeat until the design is finished.

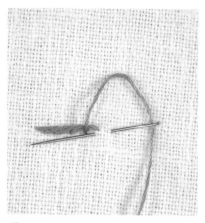

8 STEM STITCH: Working from left to right on your fabric, take a small stitch. Come up below and to the right of where you first came up. Repeat until the design is completed.

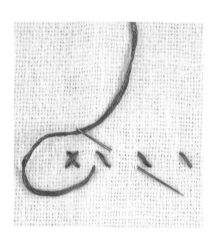

9 CROSS STITCH: Bring the needle through on the lower right line of the cross and insert a little bit up and to the left, taking a stitch through to emerge on the lower line. Working back, complete the upper section of the cross as shown. Repeat until the design is finished.

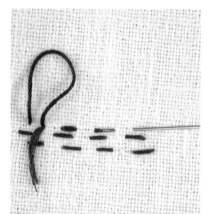

10 LINEAR RICING: Using a long running stitch, load 3–4 stitches onto the needle. Continue to stitch in somewhat even and consistent lines until the design is finished.

11 RANDOM RICING: Bring up the thread. Keeping the needle on top of the fabric, make a long running stitch. Fill the area with similar stitches in an all-over design until the pattern is finished.

#1 back stitch   #4 feather stitch   #8 stem stitch

#2 chain stitch   #5 french knot   #9 cross stitch

#3 blanket stitch   #6 running stitch   #10 linear ricing

                     #7 couching   #11 random ricing

Far East Embellishment
sashiko

Sashiko, an ancient style of embroidery from Japan, is simply a running stitch, traditionally stitched with white or natural thread on indigo cotton.

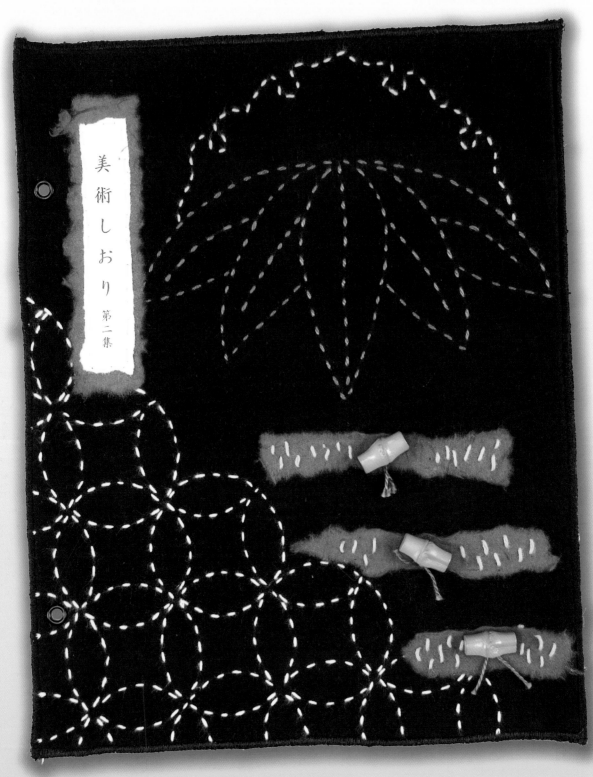

Techniques: ***Sashiko***, *Found Objects, Ricing, Attaching Paper*

sashiko

Originally, the Japanese used sashiko to hold layers of cloth together in order to have a strong product, much like quilting. It was also used to mend fabric so clothing would last longer. As fabric became less expensive and easier to obtain, sashiko became more decorative than practical. Today, sashiko is rarely used to preserve or mend fabric but, instead, beautifies everyday items such as pillows, placemats, clothing and quilts.

supplies

• Indigo blue fabric

• Sashiko thread

• Sashiko needles

• Stencils

• Chalk pencil

1 Sashiko thread comes in hanks. Untwist the hank and lay it on the table. Cut through all threads at one end.

2 Loosely braid the threads. Hold the braid at the cut ends and pull one thread from the folded end; these are the perfect length to work with.

3 Using a chalk pencil, trace the design on your fabric or use a purchased preprinted sashiko panel as shown in Step 4.

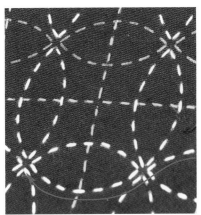

4 Sashiko motifs are designed to stitch in one direction, then back in another. To make the stitches more consistent and speed up the process, look at the pattern before stitching and map out your stitch direction.

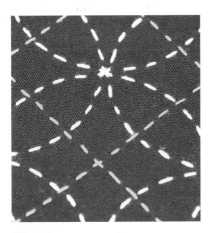

5 There are two important things to remember about sashiko. Keep the stitches even, and do not cross them over previous stitches, especially in the intersections of the design, as shown, above.

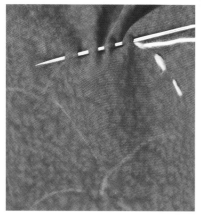

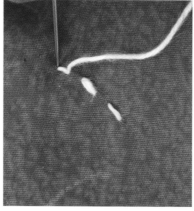

6 Start at the beginning of your map and come up from underneath. Pop the knot into the batting to hide it. Using a running stitch, load three to five stitches onto the needle and pull through. More stitches can be loaded onto the needle in the straight sections than the curved. Look ahead and plan the stitches so they do not cross over at the intersections. Continue until the thread is used up and knot off, preferably at the end of a row.

7 If the piece is going to be seen from both sides, the technique is a little different: Begin stitching in the opposite direction from the start of the design for three to four stitches. Carefully stitch back over those stitches. This will lock the thread in place. Continue until there are about 5 inches of thread left. Finish off the thread with the same technique, stitching up and back for three to four stitches. This will give a knotless piece on the back, however this is not as long lasting as when knotted.

tips

- The length of the stitch is not as important as the consistency—it is important to keep your stitches even in length and as regular as possible.

- You can use traditional quilt designs and hand-quilting thread with sashiko.

- Try using pearl cotton in different weights. When covering a large area, overlap the stencil onto the previous markings to keep it more accurate.

- Use sashiko where least expected.

- Machine-stitch sashiko designs for a fast overall background.

designer's workshop

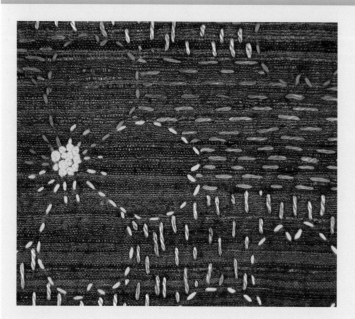

The Japanese used indigo to dye their fabric because the dye-making process involved natural ammonia, making the fabric bug resistant.

Traditionally, sashiko thread is a natural or white 100% cotton. Today, many colors are available on the market.

Sashiko needles are quite large, more the size of embroidery needles than quilting needles.

The Japanese use a small leather thimble worn on the middle finger, but a traditional quilting thimble will work as well.

Sashiko Quilt
52 x 66 inches
Ruth Chandler

Sashiko

One-Stitch Punch
ricing

Embellish a field of basic fabric with running stitches each the size of a grain of rice—hence ricing! Use ricing to create an all-over background design in a quilt or garment.

Technique: ***Ricing***

ricing

A huge selection of available weights and types of thread ensures endless effects. A good rule of thumb to remember is the heavier the thread the more the ricing will show so pick your threads accordingly. Another fun stitch to try would be the seed stitch—when 'seeding,' the size of the stitch is as small as a sesame seed.

supplies

- Top fabric
- Embroidery threads in a variety of weights
- Hand embroidery needles

1 The ricing stitch is a ¼-inch-long running stitch and the only thing to keep in mind is to try to keep the stitches even regardless of the length. There are two basic ricing stitches, random and linear. The random stitch is just as it sounds—placed in no specific order to give a piece lots of texture.

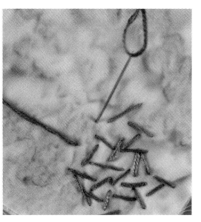

2 It is best to start the ricing from one corner of the fabric. Bring up the thread from underneath and pop the knot into the batting so it cannot be seen. Keeping the needle on top of the fabric, begin making stitches through all layers, filling the area with stitches in an all-over design.

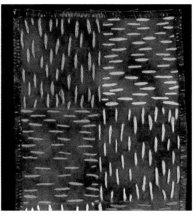

3 Linear ricing uses the same stitch as random ricing but has the stitches making lines that become the design. The lines can be marked before beginning; however, it is easy and more fun to just eyeball it and begin. The linear stitch has a more organized look and can be used as a design element.

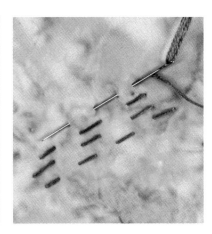

4 Bring up the thread from underneath the fabric and pop the knot through so it is buried in the batting. Using a running stitch, load 3–4 stitches onto the needle. Sometimes the thread is hard to pull through so it may be necessary to adjust the number of stitches accordingly. Continue to stitch the lines until the design is finished.

Machine Embroidery
programmed stitches

An easy way to add embellishments to a piece of fabric is to use the available stitches on the sewing machine to add a grid of simple straight stitches on a solid fabric or outline a shape on a patterned fabric.

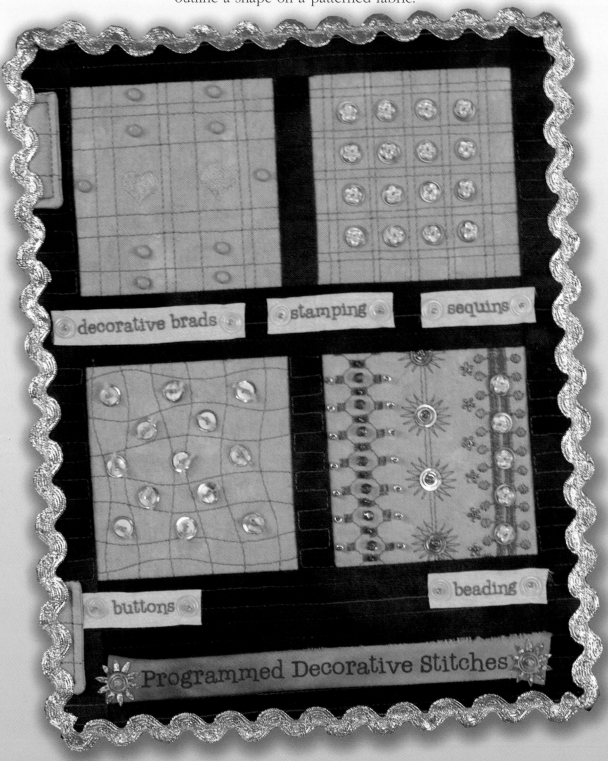

Techniques: ***Machine Embroidery****, Stamping, Brads, Buttons, Sequins, Beading*

solid fabric

Decorating a solid fabric can be as simple as using a straight or zigzag stitch or you can choose to venture further. Many sewing machines have countless stitches at the touch of a button that can add an edginess and complexity to your work without being difficult.

supplies

- Four 4-inch fabric squares
- Decorative thread
- Fusible interfacing

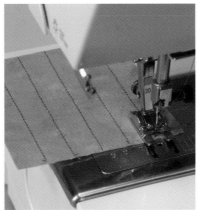

1 Stabilize the fabric squares with a light fusible interfacing. Stitch parallel, horizontal lines onto the fabric. Next, stitch parallel, vertical lines onto the fabric. Repeat to make a double-line grid.

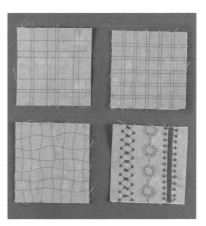

2 For variation try an irregular grid and a wavy line grid. Or, stitch a sequence of decorative stitches and then sew a mirror sequence right next to the first row. Trim the squares to 3½ inches.

patterned fabric

Enhancing a patterned fabric can be as basic as stitching close to the fabric's printed or woven design with contrasting or metallic threads and outlining or accentuating the shape of the fabric's pattern.

supplies   7-inch square of patterned fabric, a variety of decorative threads such as rayon and metallic, fusible interfacing

Techniques used in the patterned-fabric page are hand embroidery, iron-on crystals, painting, charms and sequins.

1 Stabilize the patterned fabric with a light fusible interfacing. Using a straight stitch setting, echo the design just outside the printed image.

2 Use pre-programmed leaf, feather or vine stitches to add a complexity to the existing fabric design. Trim the square to 6½ x 6½ inches.

Free Motion Embroidery
thread painting

This technique uses beautiful threads to paint your fabric, stitching everything from individual motifs to large landscapes. Thread painting adds simple embellishments to printed fabric motifs or completely fills a solid fabric with color and texture.

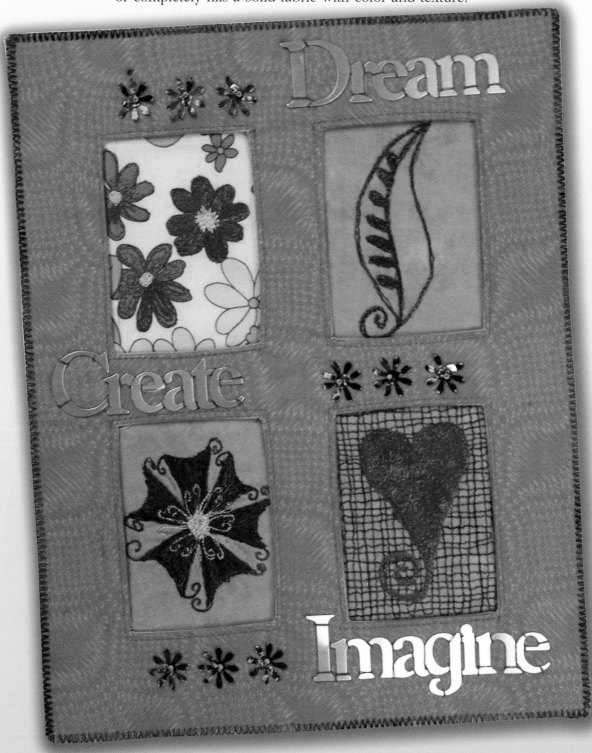

Techniques: **Thread Painting**, *Fashion a Frame, Sequins*

decorating a printed fabric

The technique requires a free-motion embroidery foot or a darning foot and lowered or covered feed dogs. Thread painting has a reputation of being difficult but with a few tips it can be easy and relaxing. To begin, just simply outline-stitch and then decorate a printed fabric motif.

supplies

- Fabrics: patterned and solid
- Machine embroidery needle
- Assorted decorative threads and lightweight bobbin thread
- Machine embroidery hoop
- Tear-away stabilizer

1 Cut pieces of printed fabric and stabilizer to fit your embroidery hoop; layer and secure in the hoop. Prepare your sewing machine for free motion stitching. Using a decorative thread in the top and a light-weight thread in the bobbin, outline-stitch your chosen motif.

2 Decide how much stitching you would like on your motif. You can stitch just a few lines to highlight the motif (lower left), lightly fill the motif with stitching that echoes the shape (center right), or fill it in completely (upper left).

open leaf design

To find images, look for simple rubber stamps, outline drawings in coloring books, nature books and catalogs. Consider tracing your own photographs, or refer to the many copyright-free design books that are available.

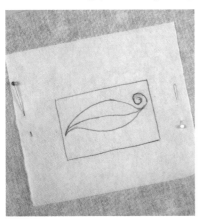

1 Ensuring all pieces are large enough for the hoop, trace a leaf onto the stabilizer. Pin the stabilizer and a plain fabric wrong sides together. Set your machine for free-motion stitching. With the stabilizer facing up and using a very fine thread in a color close to your fabric color, stitch the leaf outline.

2 Remove your work from the machine, turn it right-side up and secure in the hoop.

3 Using a decorative thread in the top and a light-weight thread in the bobbin, stitch the leaf motif, going over each line two or three times and adding a few flourishes along the center vein of the leaf.

funky flower

The thread painting process in the funky flower goes yet a step further than the open leaf in that we now fill a space, in this case a flower petal, with stitches. Also, a second color is introduced.

1 Following Step 1 on page 71, trace and then stitch a flower outline with the stabilizer facing up and using a very fine thread in a color close to your fabric. Remove this from the machine, turn the fabric right-side up and secure in the embroidery hoop.

2 Using a decorative thread in the top and a light-weight thread in the bobbin, stitch the outline of the flower shape and then add some straight stitching lines within each petal.

3 Working evenly across the entire piece, continue to fill in the petals with straight stitching. You may wish to go over each petal several times. Once the petals are filled in, re-stitch the edges of each petal and, if desired, add a curling flourish at each corner.

4 Add a flower heart by stitching in small overlapping circles with a contrasting thread and, if desired, add flourishes in the petals.

tips

- Stabilizers and hoops are helpful in controlling the most common problems of thread painting: distortion and puckering.

- When filling in areas with thread, keep in mind you are adding thread between the warp and weft threads of the fabric and only so much thread can be added before the base fabric becomes distorted.

- When you wish to create a heavily thread-painted piece choose a loosely woven fabric or fabric designed for hand embroidery such as aida cloth. As an alternative, you can stitch your design on a stabilizer base or loosely woven fabric, cut it out and appliqué it to your chosen fabric.

- Draw your own design or use drawings from coloring books, nature books and catalogs, or look for simple rubber stamps. Consider tracing photographs or refer to the many copyright-free design books available for inspiration.

heart with grid

When filling in a large motif or using stitches other than a straight stitch, a stitched grid in the motif area helps control distortion. In this example, the grid has been extended to become a design element.

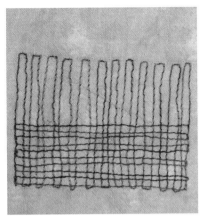

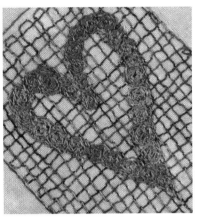

1 Following Step 1 on page 71, trace and then stitch a heart and rectangle outline with the stabilizer facing up and using a very fine thread in a color close to your fabric. Remove from the machine, turn over and secure in the embroidery hoop.

2 Using a decorative thread in the top and a light-weight thread in the bobbin, stitch a grid pattern in the rectangle.

3 Choosing a thread color to complement or blend with the grid, change the thread colors and stitch the outline of the heart. Next, stitch just inside the outline using a circular or spiraling motion.

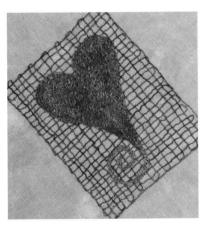

4 Using the same circular or spiraling stitch pattern, fill in the heart. You will still see open areas where the background shows. It is not necessary to completely fill in the heart—the background and grid colors add interest to the design. If desired, add a curling tail flourish.

tips

- Use a light-weight (60, 80 or 100wt.) bobbin thread. Not only does the bobbin last longer, it helps decrease bulk and fabric distortion.

- Loosen the top tension so the top thread is slightly pulled to the back of your work. This ensures you don't get dots of bobbin thread on top of your embroidery.

- If one piece of tear-away stabilizer does not offer enough support, layer it with a second piece.

- To minimize distortion, stitch over the entire design as a whole, rather than stitching one section at a time. For example, when stitching a flower, first outline the entire flower. Next, lightly fill in each petal and lastly, fill in the rest of the section.

- In thread painting, the stitch length is controlled by your machine speed and the speed you move the fabric. Experiment with the different looks of small stitches and long stitches, heavy threads and thin threads.

- Don't worry if you color outside the lines or if your stitching line goes astray. You can incorporate these wayward threads with additional stitching or remove them later.

- To avoid hand fatigue, keep the hoop in place by guiding it lightly with the fingers on the outside edges rather than gripping the hoop.

Laying Cords machine couching

Tacking down cording, ribbon, floss or braid to fabric using a second, usually thinner, thread is called couching. Depending on the machine foot used, you can couch down just about any length of fiber—even strands of beads.

*Techniques: **Machine Couching**, Hand Embroidery, Ricing*

machine couching

Traditionally done by hand, couching is a time consuming process but sewing machines make fast work of this technique. For the purpose of this exercise, whatever is being tacked down will be referred to as cording.

supplies

- Sewing machine with zigzag or decorative stitches
- Various couching feet
- Cords for couching

1 Choose a zig zag or decorative stitch that is as wide or wider than the cord. Stitch the cords onto the fabric, adjusting the stitch width as needed for each different cord.

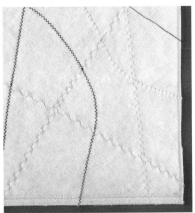

2 Viewing the workbook page from the back, and before applying the backing or further embellishments, you can see the various stitches that were used to couch the cords in place.

tips

- Experiment with all those fun stitches that never get used.

- Try all kinds of fibers, cords, ribbons or even bead strings.

- Invest in couching, or cording feet; they are well worth the additional cost.

- The great thing about couching with a sewing machine is that this can be accomplished using either a simple machine with a zig-zag stitch or a more elaborate machine with many decorative stitches. The key to successful couching is to use the right foot. The wider the cord, the wider the groove on the bottom of the foot needs to be. Some feet have multiple grooves to allow the couching of multiple cords at the same time.

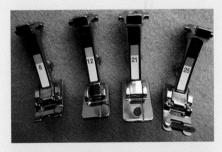

- Anything that comes in the form of a long strand can be couched, starting with threads and working up to wider and thicker cords. The only limit is the width of the groove on the bottom of the foot, which allows for control and helps keep the cord in place.

- Some feet have a slot for the cord to be threaded through and others are designed to just go over the cord, threading the cord as the foot moves over the fabric. Every model is a little different so read your machine's instructions.

- If you do not have couching feet and do not plan on purchasing them, use a standard foot with flat cords, yarns or other fibers.

Free Motion thread-lace grid

Create embellishments out of sewing thread. Delicate and open, or with fairly dense stitching, thread lace motifs can be appliquéd on top of your piece or inserted into a fabric window. Use this simple technique to create embellishments that look amazingly intricate and complex.

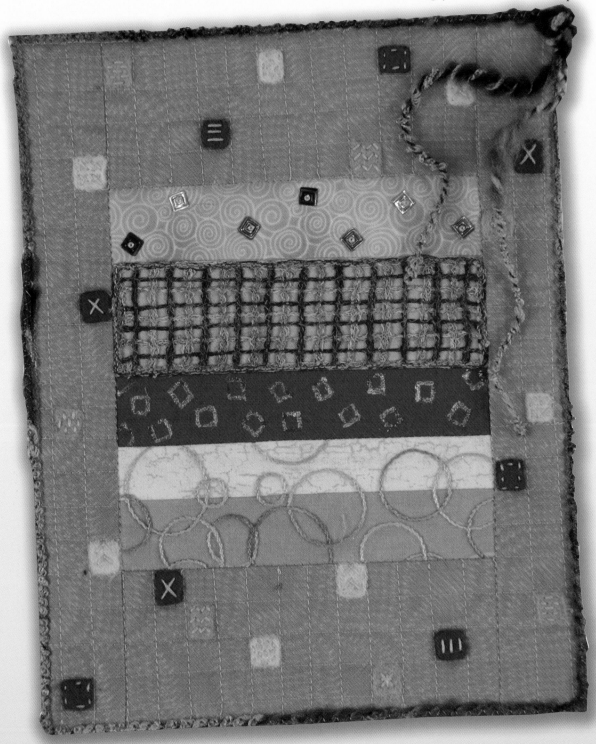

Techniques: ***Machine Lace Appliqué,*** *Needle Felting, Hand Embroidery, Foiling, Beading*

thread-lace grid

For your thread to become a piece of fabric you work in a grid system, connecting the threads with each other at multiple points so they're strong and do not fall apart once you dissolve the stabilizer. The underlying grid can be circular, triangular or organic and evenly or unevenly spaced.

supplies

- Thread in assorted colors and fibers; multi-colored threads work well and add color interest

- Clear water soluble stabilizer such as OESD AquaFilm, Sulky Solvy, or Badgemaster

- Machine embroidery hoop

- Fine-tip Sharpie and paper

1 Cut two pieces of water soluble stabilizer slightly larger than your embroidery hoop. Draw a grid design on a piece of paper. Place the stabilizer on the design and trace the design with a pen. Place the stabilizer in the hoop and tighten the hoop. Gently pull the overhanging stabilizer taut within the hoop but be careful not to stretch it.

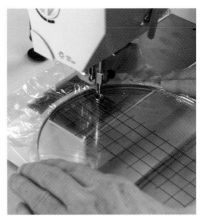

2 Drop or cover the machine's feed dogs. Position the hoop on your machine with the excess stabilizer facing up and flush with the sewing machine table. In free-motion stitching you control the length of the stitches by how fast you move the hoop.

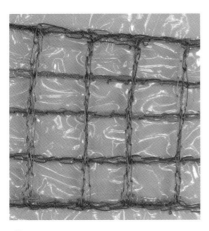

3 Stitch along the drawn pattern lines multiple times— if you want delicate lace, stitch each line 2–3 times, for thicker lace, stitch 4–5 times along each line.

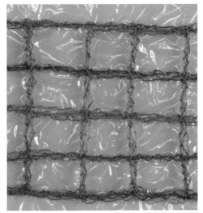

4 After stitching the lines, set your machine to a zigzag stitch with a narrow width. Remember, you control the stitch length by how fast you move your hoop. Stitch over each design line, bundling the loose threads with the zigzag stitches.

5 Change thread as desired to add multiple layers of thread to your design. When you are pleased with the stitching remove the embroidery from the hoop and trim away the stabilizer fairly close to the stitching.

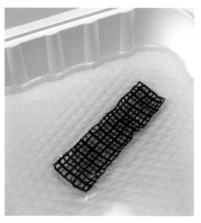

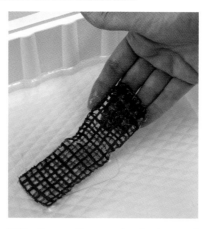

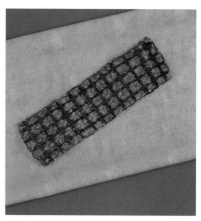

6 To dissolve the stabilizer, immerse the embroidery in a bowl of warm water, changing the water as necessary, or rinse under running water.

7 Depending on the final use of the embroidery you may want it to be soft or firm. Rinsing very briefly will retain much of the stabilizer in the threads and the piece will be firm. Repeated soaking and rinsing ensures the stabilizer is completely removed and the piece will be very soft.

8 Thread-lace embroidery can shrink so if retention of a specific shape is desired, block the embroidery on a padded surface or Styrofoam block after you've rinsed it thoroughly.

tips

- Water soluble stabilizer is available in different weights: OESD AquaFilm is light weight, Sulky Solvy is medium weight, Badgemaster and Sulky Ultra Solvy are heavy weight. A heavy weight stabilizer holds up to more stitching so choose it if you are planning on dense stitching. However, all the stabilizers can be layered and are interchangeable. When using light weight stabilizers it is best to begin with two layers.

- Save your scraps to make a liquid stabilizer, using the equivalent of approximately ¼ yard to 8 ounces water.

- When both sides of your thread-lace embroidery will be visible choose the bobbin thread with this in mind.

- Try a second, similar color to add color depth or a dissimilar color to add contrast.

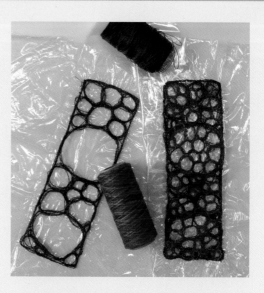

- A grid can be circular, triangular or organic and evenly or unevenly spaced.

Blue Box
11 x 6 x 2 inches
Liz Kettle

Beading

Thread-lace Grid

Machine Made
thread-lace appliqué

Use this amazing technique to create embellishments with only threads and dissolving stabilizer. Reminiscent of hand-worked needle lace, thread lace works up quickly on your machine.

*Techniques: **Machine Lace Appliqué**, Printing on Ribbon, Embroidery*

thread-lace appliqué

Using the same basic technique learned while making a thread-lace grid, create a beautiful dimensional embroidery piece that can be used as a decorative appliqué.

supplies: threads in assorted colors, Badgemaster clear water soluble stabilizer, machine embroidery hoop, fine-tip Sharpie, paper

1 Using the fine-tip Sharpie, draw a branch and leaf pattern on a piece of water soluble stabilizer—this sample was made using Badgemaster. Place the stabilizer in the hoop and tighten the hoop. Gently pull the overhanging stabilizer taut but take care not to overstretch.

2 Drop the feed dogs. Straight-stitch the branches and the outer border, going over each line about three times. It is not important to stitch exactly on the drawn line. Think of this process as sketching with your sewing machine needle.

3 Straight-stitch the leaf outlines multiple times, stitching into the branch lines and the outer border to secure the threads to its organic grid and sewing along the branches to move from leaf to leaf. Next, stitch the center and vein lines, being sure to connect the inner stitch lines to the outline.

4 Begin filling in the leaves. A looping cursive "I" stitch pattern worked between the vein stitching will ensure the threads are secured in a grid. In this sample, a bright green thread was used.

5 To add more depth to the leaves add another layer of stitching. In this sample a yellow-green thread was used. Stitch in a circular pattern over the previous layer of green thread. This last layer of stitching will hide much of the previous veining and branch definition.

6 Bring back the veining by adding another top layer of stitching; add more layers of brown stitches to thicken the branches and conceal most, but not all, the green threads. Dissolve the stabilizer in water (see page 78) and block the piece.

Wild & Woolly
needle-felting

Needle-felting is an ancient technique that has found a modern audience because it is fun, easy to do, and does not require a lot of equipment. Easily make flat or dimensional embellishments—check out the felted tube beads on page 84.

Techniques: **Needle Felting,** *Discharge Dyeing, Hand Embroidery*

needle-felting on fabric

Special barbed needles are used to mesh together fibers to create a strong fabric. You can needle-felt a variety of fibers but wool roving is most commonly used and adds great texture and color to cotton fabric. Toss needle-felted fabrics in the wash for an interesting distorted effect or do not wash if you want to keep your fabric flat.

supplies

Needle-felting needles

Wool roving in desired colors

Dense foam block

Fabric, not too tightly woven

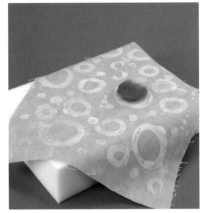

1 Place your fabric on the dense foam block. Pull wisps of wool roving from the hank and place on the area you wish to embellish. Pick up your felting needle and hold it as shown in the next photo. You may want to experiment with different holding angles to find one that suites your hand and personal technique.

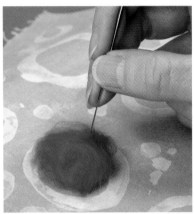

2 When pushing the needle into the fibers the needle does not need to penetrate deeply into the foam base. Try holding your finger a scant ½ inch above the tip. Your finger will act as a depth gauge. As the pile of fibers becomes matted together, move your finger slightly closer to the tip.

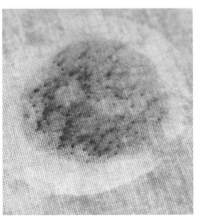

3 Pounce the needle up and down into the fibers in a random pattern. This photo shows the back of the fabric. You can clearly see how the wool roving is held in place by the fabric's woven fibers.

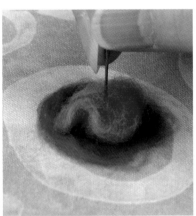

4 Continue adding fibers to cover the desired space, adding another, and maybe a third, color on top.

tips

- Felting needles are triangular or star-shaped with small barbs along the bottom portion of the shaft. These needles and barbs are very sharp.

- The needles are sized from 36 to 42 gauge—the higher the number the thinner the needle.

- Use a 36 or 38 gauge needle for overall felting and a 42 gauge needle for finishing edges and detail work.

needle-felted tube beads

Once you've mastered the art of needle-felting, graduate from flat to dimensional. Here, a simple rolled-felt bead gets some much-needed panache by adding colored polka dots and wispy lengths of roving. Another option is to blend two or more colors of roving before beginning your bead.

supplies: needle-felting needles, dense foam block, wool roving in desired colors

1 Place two to three layers of wool roving on the foam block, covering about 1 x 2-inches. Using a felting needle, mesh the layer of wool into a cohesive fabric strip. Add more wool as needed to make a fairly dense mat of wool with no holes.

2 Begin rolling up one end of the strip and secure the end to the layer by felting it in place. If your bead will be strung onto a chain or cord, make an opening by placing a length of rubber or vinyl beading cord across the strip before rolling.

3 Continue rolling the wool toward the other end, using the felting needle to mesh the fibers together.

4 To finish the ends of the bead, hold the bead upright and very carefully 'needle' the fibers down into the center to smooth out. Pounce the needle slowly and carefully in order to avoid stabbing your fingers.

5 For more excitement, add color to the bead. Felt a small amount of roving into a circle on the bead or try using a paper punch to punch out a circle of felted roving and gently pounce the circle in place on the bead.

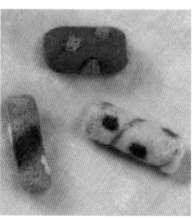

6 Lastly, embellish your bead with swirls by needle-felting a few small lengths of wool roving in different colors onto a finished bead.

Untitled
26 x 32½ inches
Lauren Vlcek

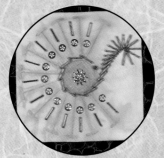

*Rusting Fabric
Beading
Iron-on Nailheads*

Quick and Easy
wool beads & silk petals

Adding depth and motion to a quilt by attaching textural elements such as wool beads and silk petals is quick and effective. Create a design with the beads or petals or enhance your fabric's flat floral or geometric design.

Techniques: ***Wool Beads and Silk Petals****, Felting, Foiling, Metal, Sequins, Beading*

wool beads & silk petals

This type of embellishing is done to a finished piece, so first construct a workbook page with four squares in different fabrics. Here, two fabrics read as solids; one fabric has a foiled flower design (see foiling on page 92), or use fabric with a flower print. A fourth fabric features a geometric pattern.

supplies

- One each 3½-inch square of four different fabrics

- Variety of silk petals (Bella Nonna brand)

- Variety of wool beads (Artgirlz brand)

- Hand-quilting thread

- Size 7 hand-embroidery needle

1 Pick five petals for the flower. Bring up the needle through the quilt, take two running stitches through a narrow petal edge, take the needle back into the fabric about ¼ inch from its exit, making sure not to go all the way through the quilt, and come back up just inside the first petal. Attach the remaining petals similarly, with a slight overlap and stitching in a small circle. Add one or two green petals for leaves.

2 Sew another silk petal flower on the foiled or printed flower square, positioning the petals so the foil or printed flower still shows in places. For additional detail, add a wool bead to the center of the flower.

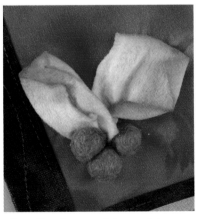

3 On the remaining solid square, stitch a few wool beads in a small cluster. Attach one or two green leaf silk petals next to the bead cluster for a sweet berries-and-leaves motif.

4 On the last fabric square, attach the wool beads in a pattern reflecting the geometric design. Other ideas may include random placement, centered, or straight or curvy lines.

  tips

- When sewing the beads and petals to a quilt square, tie a quilters knot at the end of the thread and pop it through the backing of the quilt just as you do in hand quilting so the thread will not show on the back of the quilt.

- Adding additional embellishments gives the quilt block a level of complexity and a funky-artsy appearance. Try foiling, sequins, beading, charms, or even metal.

Glitz and Glitter
angelina, textiva & crystalina

Heat-bondable fibers add magical iridescent shimmer and sparkle to your work.
Whether you want to highlight a design, cover up an ugly print or just let it shine, this
technique allows you to create fabulous glistening fabrics.

Techniques: ***Angelina, Crystalina and Textiva,*** *Brads, Sequins, Machine Embroidery, Couching*

making glistening fabric

Make a workbook page showing four types of 'fabric' you can create: The first window uses Angelina, the second Crystalina, the third features Textiva film and the fourth window shows fabric made with all three products (instructions on next page). Cut each fabric to 3 x 4 inches and cut four background pieces to the same size.

supplies

- Heat-bondable Angelina and Crystalina fibers and Textiva film in an assortment of colors

- Golden Threads Quilting Paper or one large Teflon pressing sheet or two small Teflon pressing sheets

1 Set your iron to the silk setting and cover your ironing surface with a pressing sheet or Golden Threads Paper. Spread a fine, even layer of Angelina or Crystalina fibers across the pressing surface.

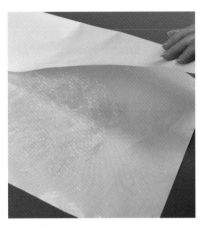

2 Fold the large pressing sheet or top the fiber layer with a second pressing sheet or more paper. Heat with the iron for approximately 10 seconds per area, keeping the iron moving slowly at all times. Pick up the sandwich, turn over and heat the other side in the same manner.

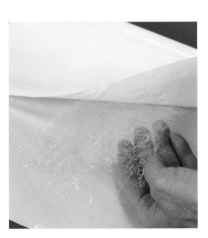

3 After the paper or pressing cloth cools, lift off the top layer and gently lift the fabric off the remaining layer. Use the fabric as is or cut into appliqués, sections for piecing or to add luminosity to a background.

product information

- Angelina and Crystalina fibers, along with the Textiva film from which they are cut, have a polyester/plastic base. Angelina fibers are cut very, very fine, straight and short, about 5 inches long. When processed they produce a soft, supple fabric. Crystalina fibers are cut with a jagged edge, are about twice as long and twice as thick as Angelina and produce a fabric that is not as soft as Angelina fabric and with more texture. Textiva looks a bit like cellophane. All three products are light reflective as well as light refractive, creating a very luminescent effect; think mother of pearl, peacock feathers or shimmering dragonfly wings.

- All three products will heat set (melt) into one another but will not attach to anything else without an iron-on adhesive or stitching. The products are machine washable on the gentle cycle; air dry.

- It is easy to control the density of the fabric you create by how much fiber you spread out on your ironing surface. A fine thin layer yields a fine thin fabric, a heavier layer yields a heavier fabric. If you want a very heavy fabric, perhaps for a base of a beaded broach, use several thinner layers rather than just one heavy layer. To make a fabric thicker, lay it on your pressing sheet, add more loose fibers, top it with a pressing sheet and heat.

combining the fibers

Combine the fibers in any way you can imagine. Here, Angelina and Crystalina fibers in the same color are meshed together; add further embellishment with a few flecks of Textiva, also in the same color.

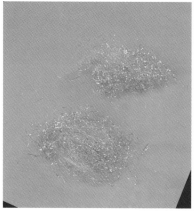

1 Set your iron to the silk setting and cover your ironing surface with a pressing sheet or Golden Threads Paper. Pull out a small handful of one or various Angelina fibers and the same amount of Crystalina fibers in the same or different colors. Lay the fibers on top of each other, then pull them apart with both hands. Lay them on top of each other again and pull them apart again.

2 Continue blending the fibers until the colors and types are well mixed; divide in two equal portions. Play with the fibers and try mixing a variety of colors.

3 Carefully spread out a fine, thin, and wispy layer of one fiber portion. Cut a few ¼ x 4-inch strips of Textiva film in one or more colors. Hold the strips together over the fiber layer and cut into ¼-inch chunks, moving around the rectangle of fibers as you cut so you get an even sprinkling of Textiva chunks.

4 If desired, dribble a shiny thread or fiber across the layer by simply unwinding the spool above the surface, letting the thread fall and curl at will and moving the spool around so you get an even amount of thread on the layer.

Take the remaining half of the fiber blend and spread out a second very fine layer on top of the first, paying careful attention to cover the shiny thread loops with bits of the fibers. For a fine, sheer fabric, don't lay the fibers on too thick. Top everything with a second layer of paper or another pressing sheet and heat for about 10 seconds per area, keeping the iron moving slowly at all times. Turn the whole sandwich over and heat the other side in the same manner. Allow the paper or pressing cloth to cool before using your new fabric.

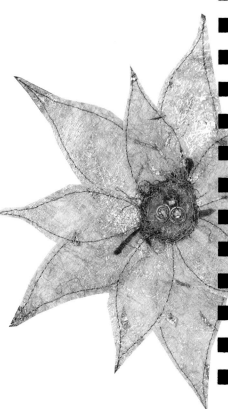

Exercise 1
8 x 10 inches
Heather Thomas

Angelina, Textiva &
Crystalina
Needle Felting
Sequins
Printing on Ribbon

Exercise 2
8 x 10 inches
Heather Thomas

Angelina & Crystalina
Rubber Stamping
Fabric Foiling
Ricing

Adding Sparkle
fabric foiling

With metallic foils the opportunities for adding glitz and sparkle to your project are limitless. Either create your own design or use a rubber stamp to apply adhesive to the fabric—then just burnish the foil in place.

*Technique: **Fabric Foiling***

fabric foiling

Fabric foil, a high-gloss mylar on a cellophane base, is available in a wide array of solid, multi- and holographic colors. Most foils are hand washable but none can handle direct heat after transfer. Foils are sold as individual rolls and in various sized multi-packs. To make your foil last longer, always cut and heat just the size you need.

supplies

- Heat-set fabric foil
- Steam-a-Seam2 adhesive
- Iron and ironing surface

1 Draw or trace a design onto the quick-release side of the product; cut out. Remove the quick-release portion and place the design on your background fabric; heat with a steam iron set on silk. Remove the top release paper.

2 Cut a piece of foil just a bit larger than your design and place on the fabric, color side up, dull silver side down. Using the side edge of your iron, bray (push) the foil onto the surface of the adhesive. As the foil adheres to the adhesive, you should be able to see the design through the foiling sheet. Place the iron down flat on top of the foil for about five seconds to heat-set it. Do not overheat the foil.

3 Allow the foil and fabric to cool. When completely cool, gently lift off an edge of the foil, then slowly pull the whole piece of foil away from the fabric. You can always add more foil. Topping one foil color with another provides a gilded, aged look. To do this, simply cut foil in a second color and repeat step 2. Be careful not to touch the first foil with the iron. Protect any areas with a Teflon pressing sheet.

- Heather used three different adhesives for her workbook sample. The bottom left square is the one featured in the instructions and uses Steam-A-Seam2. A Tonertex pen was used for the top left square, the top right square was made using a rubber stamp brushed with Foil Transfer Adhesive. The lower right square used Steam-A-Seam2 and two colors of foil.

- Steam-A-Seam2 gives you lots of control. As long as you can draw and/or cut out a design, you can use it. This adhesive is easy to use because it is sticky on both sides prior to heating.

- The Tonertex Write-n-Rub Foiling Pen yields a thin, fine line of foil. It is great for signatures or when just a tiny bit of glitz is desired. When using this product you also need to back your fabric with iron-on stabilizer such as Sulky Totally Stable.

- Foil Transfer Adhesive is specifically designed for transferring foil to fabric. It comes in a 4oz. container and has the consistency of paste. Use it when you wish to stamp your design on the fabric.

Heated Texture
Tyvek transformations

Originally a commercial product, Tyvek has been adopted into the mixed-media and crafts family because of its versatile properties. Paint it, stitch it or heat and shrink it.

*Techniques: **Tyvek Transformations**, Embossed Metal, Charms*

Tyvek

Tyvek is available by the yard from specialty sewing stores and many online suppliers or in envelope form at office supply stores. Heated with an iron or heat gun, Tyvek shrinks and distorts as it melts, providing amazing and unpredictable textures. You can stitch Tyvek to fabric, as described below, or paint with fabric paint (not acrylics as they can be very toxic when heated) and then heat to distortion to be used on the surface of a quilt.

tools & supplies

- Decorative fabric
- Tyvek
- Heat gun
- Pencil, chopstick or awl

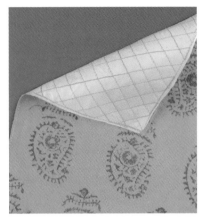

1 Cut a piece of fabric and a piece of Tyvek at least twice the size of the desired finished piece. Pin the Tyvek to the back of the fabric and stitch the two together using stipples, concentric swirls, leaves or a ½-inch grid such as the one used here. Experiment with lots of different stitches; just remember to keep it close together.

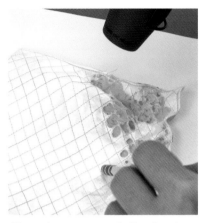

2 Place your work, Tyvek side up, on a protected surface. Grab a pencil to hold the fabric in place as it will get too hot to hold with your fingers, use a heat gun, set on a high setting, to melt the Tyvek. Hold the gun in place about 3–4 inches above the fabric until you see the Tyvek begin to melt and draw up the fabric; pull the gun away for more control of the melt. Move to the next area.

3 Try not to melt entirely through the Tyvek; leave some un-melted areas near the stitched lines. Move the gun to the next un-melted area and heat until it begins to draw up. Continue heating each area until the whole fabric is drawn up. To draw the edges over to the Tyvek side, vigorously heat them with the gun.

 designer's workshop

While you can cut shapes from fabric after it is scrunched up with heated Tyvek, you can also first stitch and cut a shape such as a circle or flower on the fabric/Tyvek combination and then heat to yield a shape with a soft, organic edge rather than a hard, cut edge.

Fast & Fun dimensional appliqué

Dimensional appliqué raises the bar, literally, as it lifts the surface of your work and adds tactile texture at the same time. Here are two methods to achieve striking three-dimensional effects.

*Technique: **Dimensional Appliqué***

dimensional appliqué—raw edge

Both the raw edge method, shown here, and the finished-edge dimensional appliqué method, shown on the following pages, can use almost any traditional hand appliqué pattern or design.

supplies

- Fabrics for background, flowers, leaves and stems
- Iron-on adhesive
- Template plastic
- Marking tool
- Basting glue
- Clover ¼-inch bias maker (optional)

1 Choose one light and one darker fabric for the flowers; cut a 10-inch square from each. Iron a 10-inch square of fusible adhesive to the wrong side of one of the fabrics. Remove the release paper from the adhesive and iron the other fabric, wrong sides together, to the first fabric. Repeat with two 8-inch squares from two green fabrics.

2 On template plastic, draw two simple flower shapes, one large and one small, and a simple leaf; cut out. Trace one small and two large flower shapes on the flower fabric for each desired complete flower. Trace one small flower for each flower bud. Trace as many leaves as desired on the leaf fabric. Cut out all the shapes just within the traced lines.

3 Using the ¼-inch bias tape maker, make ¼-inch-wide stems or make stems the old-fashioned way by ironing a strip of fabric or purchase packaged double-fold bias tape. Prepare a background for your flowers and glue-baste the bias stems in place, then add borders to your background. Layer with batting and backing. Topstitch the stems just inside the edges and quilt the background as desired.

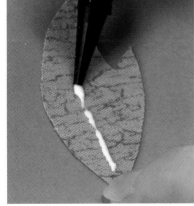

4 Form a complete flower by layering two large flowers, with petals off-set, then top with one small flower with the petals aligned with the bottom flower. Tack down each layer with basting glue. Position all of the complete flowers where desired.

5 To make a bud, fold one of the small flowers in half, then pinch the fold together to cup the bud; pin in place.

6 Position the leaves and tack down along the center with basting glue. Stitch each leaf center with matching thread and, if desired, add veins. Load machine with thread to accent the flowers and stitch a starburst design in the center of each flower and a half starburst at the base of each bud.

Outstanding Option
dimensional appliqué

Create floral fabrications that leap off your quilt, made possible by a light layer of batting that adds dimension to your flower petals and leaves. This time-tested embellishing technique is quite evident in the classic Baltimore Album quilt.

*Technique: **Dimensional Appliqué***

dimensional appliqué—finished edge

Adding volume to appliqué is one way to add dimension to your work. Here, you accomplish this effect by adding batting to and finishing the edges of petals and leaves. The edges are finished so when you manipulate the flower components they stay firm and crisp, allowing for a realistic depiction.

supplies

- Fabrics for background, flowers, leaves and stems
- Stamens
- Scraps of very thin batting
- Permanent fabric glue
- Clover ¼-inch bias tape maker (optional)
- Spray starch
- Small, pointy scissors or awl
- Point-turning tool
- Template plastic
- Straight pins
- Marking tool
- Basting glue

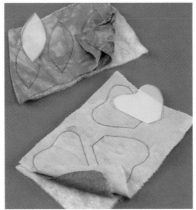

1 Draw a petal and a leaf design onto template plastic and cut out. Cut two 8-inch squares of fabric for the flowers, one light and one darker. Trace the petal template eight times to the wrong side of one of the fabrics, leaving ½-inch space in between. Place the fabrics with right sides together, traced designs on top, on a piece of batting and pin through all three layers. Repeat with two 6-inch squares of fabric for three leaves.

2 Machine-sew on the traced line around each shape, overlapping the stitches at the beginning and end to secure. Cut out each shape with a ⅛-inch seam allowance. Being careful not to cut through both layers of fabric, cut a small opening in the back of each petal and leaf.

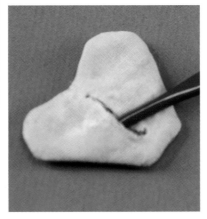

3 Using a point-turning tool, carefully turn each petal and each leaf right side out. You should have eight petals and three leaves.

4 Whipstitch the openings closed with matching thread. Prepare the stems and the workbook page as described in Step 3 on page 97.

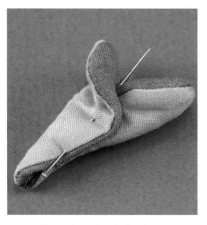

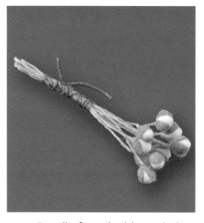

5 To make a bud, fold the petal edges toward the center; pin to secure and tack together with matching thread.

6 Bundle four double-ended stamens and fold in half. Twist the folded end and wrap with thread; knot off. Insert the tip of your permanent glue down into the bud, squeeze out a little bit of glue, then insert the folded end of the stamens into the bud. Glue or tack down the buds.

7 Pinch the edges of two petals at the bottom and stitch in place. Using permanent fabric glue, glue down the two pinched petals with a bit of glue under each end. Bundle eight double-ended stamens and fold in half. Twist the folded end and wrap with thread; knot off. Position and whipstitch in place.

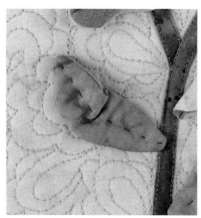

tips

- Set your machine for short stitches so when you turn your leaves or petals right side out the seam does not show.

- Keep all your appliqué pieces—finished or unfinished petals, leaves, stamens, etc.—in a zippered plastic bag until you need them.

8 Place the remaining petal on top of the stem so it covers up the folded ends of the stamens and is snug up against the two lower petals; glue in place and secure with hidden stitches.

9 Using matching thread, sew a running stitch up the center of each leaf; exit through the back of the leaf and gently gather the thread to draw up the leaf, making it curl. When you are pleased with the way it is curling up, secure the thread on the back of the leaf. Position the leaves and glue in place or tack down with hidden stitches.

Feeling Blue
45 x 60 inches
Heather Thomas

Foiling

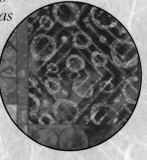

Rubber Stamping

Create Whimsy
going for glitter

Microfine glitter powder adds a touch of unconventional whimsy to your fabric and enhances a pattern with very little effort. Available in a huge array of vibrant colors, glitter is an effective last-minute embellishing product.

Techniques: ***Going for Glitter,*** *Charms*

going for glitter

There are many different glitter products on the market. Be sure to look for one that is labeled cosmetic or make-up grade which is so fine it is hard to see the individual glitter pieces. Make-up grade glitter will give you a very elegant result whereas other, less fine, products may have a less refined look.

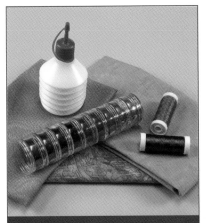

supplies

* Cosmetic-grade glitter in an assortment of colors

* Clear-drying permanent fabric glue

1 Using permanent, clear-drying fabric glue, outline an existing fabric design or pattern, as shown here, or draw your desired design to your base fabric. Another option is to apply glue to a stamp and then applying the stamp to the fabric.

2 While the glue is still wet, pour glitter over the drawn design and let set for at least 15 minutes.

3 Very carefully pick up the fabric—try not to crease it—and pour the excess glitter back into the container.

4 Set the design aside to dry for several hours or overnight. Once completely dry, hold the fabric over a trash can and gently pat the backside to remove any excess glitter.

product info

• Another option for applying glue to the fabric is to use the Tonertex Glue Pen which gives you a very thin line of glue.

• Iron some iron-on stabilizer to the back of your fabric following the manufacturer's instructions. Remove the cap from the pen and press the tip into a piece of scrap fabric to start the flow of the glue. Draw a design directly on the surface of the fabric, making sure that you have a visible line of glue (it should be slightly raised above the surface of the fabric); let dry for 10-15 minutes or until it is still tacky to the touch.

• Dab your fingertip into the glitter (in dry climates it may be necessary to wet your finger first) and gently rub the glitter into the glue. Add more glitter to your fingertip and to the fabric as needed. Keep rubbing glitter into the glue until the design is completely covered.

Foam

hard embellishments

Hard embellishing techniques demand attention and feature

those unique items that take our projects out of the traditional sewing

and quilting arena and into the purely decorative world of art.

Beads and crystals add sparkle and texture. Metal, silk cocoons

and rods bring an unexpected element and delightful contrast to

fabric. Found objects, charms and paper offer a chance to record

your personal journey. Explore these techniques to find the ones that

help convey your story or just embellish your work.

"Some may say 'Less is more' or even 'More is more' but
I say 'More is never enough!'"

Lauren Vlcek

Adding Adornment
beads galore

Add beading to quilts, garments or accessories to make them uniquely yours.
First, sew beads to accent a printed pattern such as the Single Stitch, shown below,
then progress to following your own design path.

Techniques: **Beading,** *Printing on Ribbon, Couching*

beads galore

Usually, the eye is fascinated by textures and multi-colored effects and stimulated by novelty—iridescent, opalescent, and metallic finishes are especially arresting. To complete all four beading techniques, construct a four-block workbook page, but layer just the top and batting, saving the backing for last. (See page 8.)

supplies

- Eight 3½-inch fabric squares
- Silamide beading thread
- Size 10 beading needles
- Seed beads, size 6, 8, and 11
- Bugle beads in any size or length
- Novelty beads such as leaves, flowers or drops

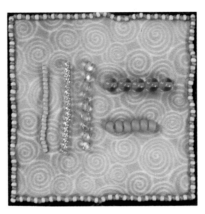

COUCHING: Tack down a string of beads onto a background to avoid gapping, sagging or hanging.

1 Trace or draw the line of your design to the fabric. Knot a length of Silamide thread and bring the needle through to the right side of your work at your starting point. String as many size 11 seed beads on the thread as you need to cover the design line.

2 Lay the strung beads on the fabric along the design line with first bead against the thread at its exit point and without any gaps. Bring the needle down through the fabric, directly at the end of the bead line, and secure with a tiny stitch.

3 Go back and come up three to four beads from the end; take a stitch over the thread between the beads to secure the bead line. Continue taking small stitches, looping over the thread every three to five beads to keep the bead line securely in place. Knot off when you are back to the starting point.

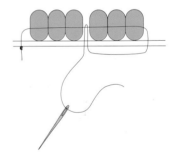

BACKSTITCH: This is used to make a long line of beads and is great for outlining shapes or objects.

1 Knot the thread and bring the needle up at the starting point. Tug on the thread to pop the knot into the batting. String three (size 8 or larger) or five (size 11) beads onto the thread. Holding the thread taut, gently push the beads back with the needle so they press against the fabric at the starting point. Reinsert the needle into the quilt right behind the last bead so the beads do not gap (too long a distance) or pucker (too short a distance).

2 Take a small backstitch, backing up one bead if you strung three, or two beads if you strung five, taking care not to pierce the thread. Go through the last previously laid bead(s), then add three to five more beads to the thread and repeat from the beginning of this step until the line is completed; knot off.

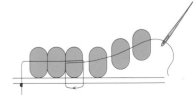

BUGLE STITCH: Use for elaborate lines and swirls. Bugle beads have broken ends which can easily cut thread. To avoid this, place a seed bead at each end of a bugle bead to prevent thread from contacting the rough edge of the bead.

1 Knot the thread and bring up the needle at the starting point. String one size 11 seed bead, a bugle bead, and another size 11 seed bead. Holding the thread taut, push back gently on the strung beads to direct them into place and to gently push them against the fabric at the starting point. Reinsert the needle directly after the last seed bead and bring it back up right next to the previous starting point. Repeat as many times as desired.

2 Next, vary the placement of the beads to form curves or long thin lines. This is a most fun stitch to play with due to the wandering nature of the stitch so try several different approaches.

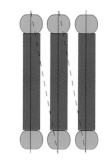

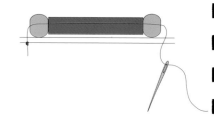

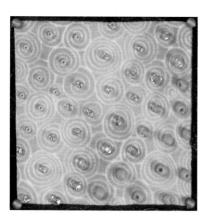

SINGLE STITCH: Makes a highlight dot or use as a textural element. It is a great, simple stitch for tiny embellishing details.

1 Knot the thread and bring up the needle at the starting point. String a single bead. Reinsert the needle next to the bead and come back up through the fabric at the point of the next stitch; repeat as desired.

NOTE: If the stitches are fairly far apart it is better to knot off the thread between each stitch.

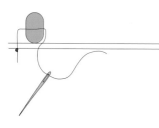

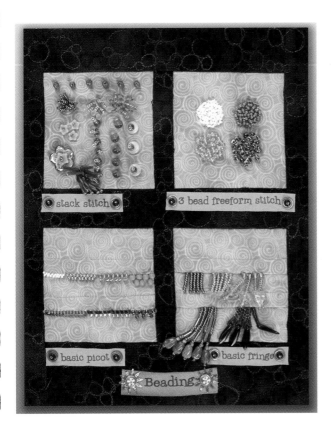

stack stitch

3 bead freeform stitch

basic picot

basic fringe

Beading

intricate beading

Once you have the simple beading methods under control read the introduction on the next page and then make another four-square workbook page to try your hand at more intricate beading stitches, including a few very pretty finishing stitches for edges.

STACK STITCH: Use for a grass-like texture, hair and shaggy textural effects when packed closely to other stacked stitches.

1 Knot the thread and bring up the needle at the starting point. String three or four seed beads. Skipping the last bead you strung, go back down through the stack of beads and the fabric. Come back up through the fabric at the point of the next stitch; repeat.

NOTE: The top bead is called a 'turn-around bead' and will hold the other beads in the stack. Pull the thread tight so the turn-around bead stands on its side.

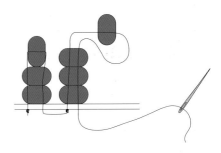

THREE-BEAD FREEFORM STITCH: A textural stitch, terrific for fluffy items such as clouds or moss.

1 Knot the thread and bring up the needle at the starting point. String three size 8 or 11 seed beads. Take the needle to the back, one bead width away from where it came up; the stitch distance should be about the same size as one of the beads used for the stitch. (Later play with a variety of sizes to see what happens.)

2 Gently pull the thread to make the middle bead stand up. Repeat these steps until the desired area is filled in.

NOTE: The stitch placement should be a bit haphazard for a random, somewhat bubbly, look to the beaded area.

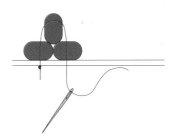

Use the next two techniques to embellish fabric edges. Woven fabrics must have a finished edge as an unfinished edge will fray and release the beading. Sew two ½-inch-deep tucks in two 3½-inch squares to serve as sample edges. These stitches work well on ultra-suede and felt which do not need to be hemmed.

BASIC PICOT STITCH: A simple edge stitch that adds a fun textural element to pleats, tucks, and bindings. It is particularly effective with two different colors or sizes of beads.

1 At the edge of a tuck take a small stitch from back to front. String a single size 8 seed bead.

2 Again, bring the needle from back to front in the same place as the first stitch, and then string a seed bead.

3 String a size 11 seed bead and a size 8 seed bead. Bring the needle from back to front of the tuck next to the already attached bead, bring the needle up through the hole of the size 8 bead ONLY (this is the bead that is closest to the fabric edge). Repeat all along the edge as desired.

NOTE: Play with different bead sizes and colors for different looks. If the stitches between beads are too close, the edge will ruffle. If the stitches between beads are too far, the edging will have gaps.

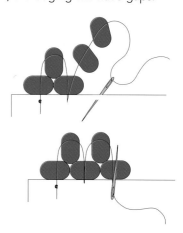

BASIC FRINGE: Basic fringe provides your work with movement and action.

1 Knot the thread and come up from back to front. String a variety of beads to the desired fringe length. The last bead is the 'turn-around' bead— make it a leaf, drop or flower bead.

2 Skipping the last bead, go back through the rest of the beads and the fabric edge or quilt, holding the last bead with one hand while pulling the thread to adjust the tension of the fringe.

3 Knot off at the base of each fringe so if it catches and breaks, only one fringe will be lost. Knotting off each time also keeps an even tension in each fringe. Repeat until the desired fringed effect is achieved.

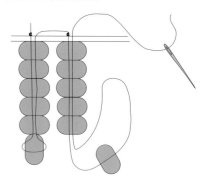

Every blade of grass has its fairy
that bends over it
and whispers,"Grow, Grow."

Green Fairy
10 x 14 inches
Lauren Vlcek

Deconstructed Crazy Quilting
Fashion a Frame
Machine Embroidery
Couching
Beading
Sequins

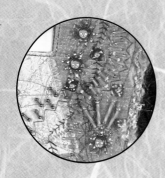

glitz & glitter
mini marbles

Tiny marbles, also known as micro, or no-hole, beads, adhere to your fabric similar to glitter. Basically, you are drawing with glue and adding beads for a unique effect.

*Techniques: **Mini Marbles**, Machine Embroidery*

mini marbles

These teeny tiny beads come in several sizes and many colors. Here, the .5mm size was used which is available in more than 20 colors. You can generally find the beads with the scrapbooking supplies.

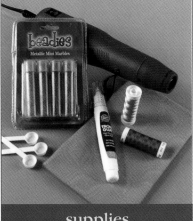

supplies

- Micro beads in various sizes and colors
- Dries Clear fabric adhesive
- Heat gun
- Bead scoop or teaspoon
- Sheet of paper

tips

- Use a needle dipped in glue to make a fine glue line.
- Mix bead sizes to give more texture.
- Omit glue in parts of the design to give the illusion of shape.
- The beads are very small so make sure to work on a flat solid surface.
- Use stencils for a great design.
- Micro beads make terrific flower centers.
- Remember, sometimes less is more—the illusion of shape gives a great effect.
- If desired, quilt the fabric before adding the beads.

1 Prepare your quilt sandwich. Draw or trace a design on the top fabric.

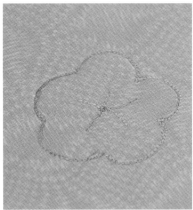

2 Stitch on the drawn or traced lines to provide a channel for the beads.

3 Working with only one bead color or size at a time, trace a stitched line with glue.

4 Spoon up beads in the desired color or size and pour them onto the glue; let dry.

5 Crease a sheet of paper, pick up your work and gently shake the excess beads onto the paper. Slide the beads from the paper back into their container.

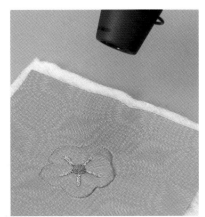

6 Repeat Steps 1–5 with each color and size bead until your design is complete. Set the beads with a heat gun; do not skip this or the beads may come off.

Charming Additions
sequins, charms & more

Add novelty to your fabric with items that help express the concept of your
artwork and have special meaning to you such as old buttons,
charms, jewelry pieces, scraps of metal and found objects.

*Techniques: **Sequins, Charms & More**, Printing on Ribbon*

sequins, charms, buttons and found objects

To complete all four of the following techniques, construct a four-block workbook page, but layer just the top and batting, saving the backing for last (see Instructions on page 8).

supplies

• Four 3½-inch fabric squares

• Silamide beading thread

• Size 10 beading needles

• Sequins, charms and buttons in a variety of colors and shapes

• Found objects (vintage game pieces, small metal washers, pins, etc.)

SEQUINS: Sequins are available in an array of colors, finishes, sizes and shapes.

Stack Stitch With Sequins is a variation on the Bead Stack Stitch, see page 109, where one or more sequins combine with a single bead or with several beads in a stack. Try a large sequin topped with medium and small sequins as well as a bead or two.

CHARMS: Charms impart a message and add movement.

To attach a charm, knot the thread, bring the needle up to the right side, through the hole of the charm, and stitch down with several stitches; knot off on the back. For variety, tie the charm in place with decorative thread and a bow or knot on top, or stack-stitch a few beads on top of the charm hole.

FOUND OBJECTS: By definition, found objects are unique and not available commercially, yet they can be 'found' just about anywhere. Look for old game pieces, watch parts, small jewelry pieces, small bits of discarded hardware,

and even natural finds such as twigs and seedpods. Many found objects are available in the scrapbooking isle of craft and hobby stores and although not authentic found objects, they can have a similar effect and are very easy to 'find.'

To attach, you can drill a hole through a found object or, especially if it is metal or stone, you can couch it in place. Usually this type of embellishment is put on fabric that will not be washed, such as a wall hanging or art quilt.

BUTTONS: Buttons are the traditional embellishing workhorses.

Attach them in the usual manner or apply with specialty thread or cording tied on top. For a bolder statement stack a few buttons.

No-Sew Glow
iron-on crystals

Nothing works better to make your project shine than a bit of glitz.
Crystals and nailheads in all shapes, sizes, and colors add
gloss and glamour and easily affix to your fabric using your iron.

Techniques: ***Iron-on Crystals,*** *Printing on Ribbon*

iron-on crystals

Sometimes referred to as hot-fix crystals, these tiny items are not actually limited to just crystals but also comprise small metal embellishments in a wide range of shapes and finishes. They are used in a similar fashion to beads or sequins but their application does not involve sewing so they are quick and simple to use.

supplies

- Hot-fix crystals and small brass nailheads

- Small Clover brand iron or regular iron

- Fine-tipped tweezers

1 Iron-on crystals are applied to a finished piece so begin by making a single-block workbook page (see page 8). Place a crystal or nailhead, flat side down, on the fabric.

2 Gently press a hot iron on the crystal for a few seconds to activate the glue. Allow the area to cool. If the crystal did not stick repeat the process. Attach the nailheads in the same manner.

 designer's gallery

Sculptural Fabric Beads
24 x 12 inches
Heather Thomas

Pronged Approach decorative brads

Usually found in the scrapbooking section of the crafts store, brads come in many different sizes, colors, and letter and symbol shapes. Select those that enhance the theme of your project.

Techniques: **Decorative Brads,** *Printing on Ribbon, Sequins*

decorative brads

Use brads by themselves as an embellishment or use them to attach other embellishments to fabric such as the printed-ribbon words on this workbook page, left. To have a finished back on your workbook page, layer just the top and batting, then apply the brads, saving the backing for last. (See page 8.)

supplies

- Decorative brads
- Awl

1 Using an awl, poke a hole completely through the quilt or fabric layers at the brad's desired location.

2 Remove the awl and place the brad in the hole left by the awl.

3 On the backside of your work, spread the prongs of the brad until they lay flush with the backing. Repeat as needed.

4 To attach an embellishment with a brad, use an awl to poke a hole completely through the quilt at the desired

location. If the embellishment is made of fabric, align it and pierce it along with the quilt. If the embellishment is a charm or other item with an existing hole, place the brad into the hole of that embellishment with the right side of the brad and the right side of the embellishment facing up. Remove the awl from the quilt and push the brad in the hole left by the awl. Spread the prongs at the back of the quilt until they lay flush with the backing of the quilt. Repeat as needed.

Venturing Out
make mine metal

Metal may be the last thing you think of when embellishing your quilt but it is fun to work with and has many exciting uses. With a bit of caution, a small stash of old sewing-machine needles and a pair of old scissors, metal adds a new technique for you to try.

*Techniques: **Metal**, Wool Beads, Couching*

metal

Metal is available in thin foils and in thicker sheets—the higher the gauge the thinner the sheet. Metal with a gauge between 40 and 36 is great for embossing and sewing and easily cuts with scissors or a rotary cutter. Metal foils and sheets are readily available in aluminum, copper and pewter and a multitude of colors. Colored metal is generally made from aluminum; one side has color, the reverse is aluminum.

supplies

- Assorted metal, including aluminum or copper foil, 40- to 36-gauge metal sheet, hardware cloth and colored metal

- Wire cutters and scissors or rotary cutter and mat

- Embossing tool or mechanical pencil with no graphite

- Emery board or sandpaper

- Thread and old machine needles (size 90 embroidery needles or topstitch needles work well)

- Assorted fabrics and acrylic felt

- Heavy duty stabilizer such as Pellon Heavy Weight or Peltex

- Fusible Web such as Misty Fuse

CHECKERBOARD SQUARE

1 Cut a 4-inch square of aluminum. Using a ruler and embossing tool or mechanical pencil with no graphite, score a ½-inch grid.

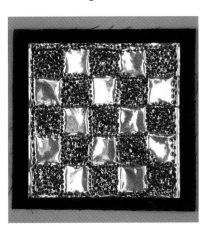

3 Set your sewing machine for free-motion stitching and

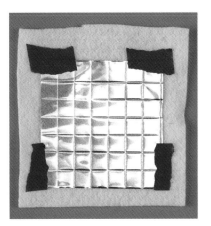

2 Place the gridded aluminum square on a 5-inch piece of stabilizer. Secure with masking or double stick tape.

load with thread in your desired color. Beginning in the center square and using a straight free-motion stitch, move the metal in small circular movements to fill in the square. Repeat every other square until you are one square from the edge all around. Stitch along the grid lines to highlight the grid pattern and outline the stitched squares. Trim the stabilizer. Using scissors or a rotary cutter, cut the metal just beyond the last stitched squares. Sew the piece to a slightly larger piece of felt.

 designer's workshop

Ribbon made of metal is as cool as it sounds. It is a tubular ribbon knit from fine metal threads; it can be manipulated and stitched, plus you can insert beads or other fibers inside the tube. Here, simply stretch the ribbon at random intervals and stitch down using a free-motion straight stitch.

THREE-SQUARE SQUARE

1 Cut a 4-inch piece of metal. Crumple, twist and bend the metal square with your hands but avoid crumpling too much or the metal will tear.

2 Smooth out the metal with your fingers. Using the emery board or sand paper, gently remove color from the raised, crumpled ridges. Cut the piece to 3 inches square.

3 Cut a 3-inch square of aluminum foil or candy wrapper and a 4-inch square of stabilizer. Fuse foil to stabilizer with fusible web.

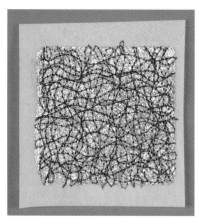

4 Set your machine for free-motion stitching and stitch over the foil in a meandering straight stitch. Turn the stitched piece 90 degrees and stitch curving lines in the other direction, creating an organic grid effect.

5 Cut three small squares from the stitched foil and glue them to the sanded metal square. Edge-stitch the crumpled square to a piece of felt.

 tips

- Always stitch metal with a piece of fabric, felt or stabilizer underneath in order to protect your machine surface from potential scratches.

- Save old machine needles for use with metal. Discard needles after sewing on metal. A size 14/90 embroidery or topstitch needle works well.

- Use double stick tape to secure metal to stabilizers or fabric while stitching.

- Fusible web products work well on metal but keep in mind that metal will absorb heat. Allow to cool before touching.

- Use a longer stitch length and sew slower than normal.

- Metal sheet and foil can be cut with a rotary cutter, ruler and mat or scissors.

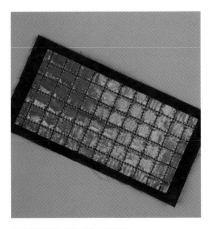

GRIDDED RECTANGLE

1 Cut a 2¾ x 6-inch piece of colored metal and a 3½ x 7-inch piece of fabric. Fuse the metal to the fabric with fusible web. Stitch a ½-inch grid pattern on the fused layers.

2 Cut a ¾ x 5-inch strip of colored metal and secure a slightly smaller piece of stabilizer to the back with double stick tape. Bend the piece in half (metal to metal) to crease the center of the metal strip. Fold out the creased metal.

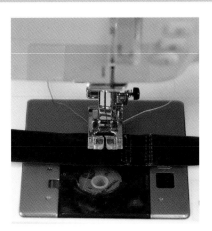

3 Beginning just to one side of the crease, straight-stitch three lines across the width of the metal, very close together. Slide the metal over approximately ¼ inch using the edge of your presser foot as a measuring tool. Continue stitching groups of three lines to the left and right of the crease to the end of the metal. Remove from machine.

4 Using a metal ruler or similar sharp-edge tool, bend the metal into an accordion fold at the end of each stitched section.

5 Using wire cutters, cut a 1½ x 4¼-inch piece of hardware cloth. Attach the stitched metal strip, stabilizer-side down, to the hardware cloth with hand stitches. Stitching through the stabilizer only, catch the indented fold of the strip, wrap the thread around the hardware cloth wires and continue to the next indented fold. Stitch along both sides and the ends.

6 With the stitched metal strip facing color-side up, center the hardware cloth on the gridded rectangle; hand-sew at the short ends to secure. Place the assembled piece on your fabric and stitch around the edges.

Vintage Vision
embossed metal

Try your hand at embossed metal with a twist. And did you ever imagine you would transfer an image to metal and then sew it to your quilt? The photo-transfer results in a print reminiscent of vintage daguerreotype pictures.

Techniques: ***Metal Collage***, *Machine Embroidery, Foiling, Buttons*

embossed metal

Emboss a motif or word into metal and then, to prevent the embossed areas from collapsing, fill them with spackle. Making a picture on metal is easier than it seems when you use Transfer Artist Paper.

supplies

- Sheet of aluminum, between 36 and 40 gauge

- Old mouse pad or mat made for embossing metal

- Firm surface for refining such as acrylic mat or cutting mat

- Embossing tools such as a Teflon or wooden stylus or the rounded end of a fine-art paint brush

- Refining tool such as a large wooden bamboo skewer or a tool made specifically for refining

- Paper stumps

- Prepared drywall spackle

- Double-stick tape and masking tape

- Heavy stabilizer such as Pellon Heavy Weight or Peltex, or two layers of light weight stabilizer

- Embossing mold

- Image printed on Transfer Artist Paper (see page 42)

- Word printed on paper in mirror image

- Hand dyed vintage linen, trim and other fabrics as desired

1 Prepare your base: Secure vintage linen fabric and trim to base fabric. Using a rotary cutter, ruler and cutting mat, cut a piece of metal ½ inch larger than the image you have printed. Transfer the image onto the metal (see Transfer Artist Paper image directions on page 42). Determine placement on your collage and stitch the metal image in place.

2 For the embossed corner, cut a metal triangle slightly larger than one diagonal half of the decorative mold you have chosen. Bend the short metal edges over the mold edges and tape the diagonal edge in place with masking tape. Using a large paper stump, rub over the metal to reveal the mold pattern, continuing with smaller paper stumps to further refine the pattern.

3 Remove the metal from the mold. Using a palette knife, gently apply spackle to the back of the metal triangle, filling in the embossed pattern. Use a light touch so you do not crush the embossed lines.

4 Use an old credit card to even out the spackle and to fully fill the embossed lines; let the spackle dry. Trim the embossed image; secure to the fabric collage with double stick tape and stitch along the edge using a zipper foot.

125

5 Cut a 2 x 5-inch piece of metal. Decide on a poignant word for your collage. Use your word processing program to print the word in mirror image or write the word on paper and hold it up to a well-lit window to trace the word in reverse on the back of the paper. Tape the word to the back of the metal.

6 Place the metal face down on an embossing mat or old mouse pad. Use an embossing tool to trace the word to the back of the metal. Once traced, cut your metal to size.

7 Turn the metal over and place on a firm surface such as an acrylic mat. Outline the letters with a refining tool. Use the paper stump to further shape and define the letters.

8 Using a palette knife, apply spackle to the back of the metal, filling in the embossed letters; let dry. Cut a piece of heavy stabilizer ¼ inch larger all around than the embossed metal. Secure the metal to the stabilizer with double stick tape. Set your machine for a decorative stitch and stitch along the top and bottom of the metal with a curved line.

9 Using old scissors, trim the metal along the stitched lines. Sew the embossed word in place on your collage, using, if necessary, a zipper foot to avoid the raised letters.

tips

SAFETY PRECAUTION

- When stitching on metal, use an old sewing machine needle and wear eye protection.

Blueberry
10 x 22 inches
Heather Thomas

Found Objects
Beading

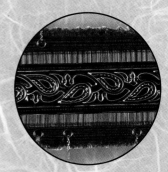

Embossed Metal

Photo Transfer

Five Ways
attaching paper

You've embellished with beads and buttons, fibers and foiling—how about giving paper a try?
Here are several methods for attaching paper to fabric, each one more decorative than the other.

*Techniques: **Attaching Paper**, Buttons*

attaching paper

Choose a sheet of decorative paper with interesting motifs and cut into various squares and rectangles. Arrange the paper pieces on your fabric and secure in place with fusible web, then choose your attachment method.

supplies

- Decorative paper
- Fusible web
- Assortment of thread
- Stapler
- Eyelets and eyelet setter
- Hand sewing needles
- Decorative buttons
- Ribbon
- Clear drying glue and a toothpick

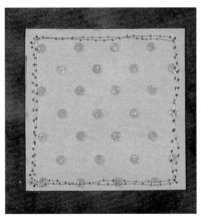

MACHINE STITCHING
Using a longer than normal straight or decorative stitch, sew along the edges of the paper once or twice.

EYELETS
Attach a piece of paper using eyelets. Thread a decorative ribbon through the eyelet holes.

BUTTONS
Using a decorative thread, sew a button at each corner; tie the thread ends on top of the button. Using a toothpick, place a dot of glue on the knot to secure.

HAND SEWING
With thick thread or embroidery floss in a sharp needle, stab-stitch along the paper edges with a straight or decorative stitch. Take care not to tear the paper.

STAPLES
First, make a thread bundle. Double about a yard of thread on itself, repeat twice or three times until you have a 4- to 5-inch bundle. Tie a knot in the center of the thread bundle; make three more bundles. In each corner, staple the paper to the fabric,

catching the thread bundle under the staple near the knot. Bring the thread ends together and tie a knot on top of the staple. Hold the thread ends together and clip them to the desired length. Use the toothpick or skewer to place a dot of glue on the thread knot to secure it.

Stitching Ephemera
nine-patch sampler

Create a nine-patch paper-on-fabric sampler using as many different types of paper as you can find. Consider altering the paper color using colored pencils or watercolor paints and try different attachment techniques.

Techniques: **Nine-Patch Sampler,** *Hand Embroidery, Beads*

nine-patch sampler

To begin, tear bits of paper along a ruler for a nice deckled edge, cut with a decorative-edge scrapbooking scissors, or use as is. Layer the tiny bits of paper until you have a pleasing composition and then secure to the fabric with decorative machine and hand-sewing stitches.

supplies

- Assorted papers such as bags, maps, napkins, Grungeboard, found papers, paper flowers, candy wrappers, art paper, etc.

- Fusible web

- Assortment of thread and hand sewing needles

- Small piece of acrylic felt

 designer's workshop

Like many mixed-media artists, Liz cannot bear to throw out even the tiniest scrap of paper. Wrappers from her favorite chocolates, stamps off letters from far-way friends, and tickets to memorable events all are saved for future use. To help you get started, and for suggestion only, Liz explains which types of papers she used for each square.

1 Square cut from a paper bag from Starbucks, secured with free motion zigzag stitching; two paper flowers secured with beads in the center.

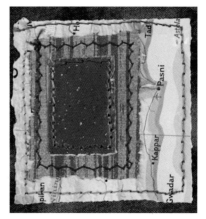

2 Piece of a map layered with a piece of torn napkin and a bit of paper from a chocolate wrapper, secured with free-motion straight and zigzag stitching.

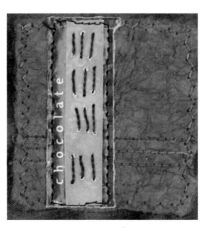

3 Crinkled art paper, secured with decorative and free-motion zigzag stitching. Strip of decorative paper layered on a chocolate wrapper sewn on top and hand embroidered.

4 Paint-sample card layered with decorative tissue paper and torn dictionary page pieces stained with a watercolor paint, secured with straight machine stitching.

5 Torn dictionary page piece stained with watercolor paint, layered with lacy tissue paper and a gold-painted Grungeboard heart sewn in place with free-motion straight and zigzag stitches.

6 Metallic interior of tea bag wrapper and outside of tea bag wrapper, stitched down with free-motion straight and zigzag machine stitching; topped with two paper flowers attached with French knots.

7 Metallic chocolate wrapper, a canceled postage stamp and art paper, secured in place with free-motion straight and zigzag stitching.

8 Chocolate wrapper, trolley ticket (which turned completely black when ironed) and decorative art paper, stitched with free motion straight and zigzag stitches.

9 Paper napkin fused to a piece of acrylic felt and decorative straight stitching added; gold tissue paper and painted dictionary page secured with free-motion straight and zigzag stitching.

 tips

- Most decorative paper napkins are 2-ply. To use, first separate the top printed layer from the plain bottom layer.

- When using thin paper napkin layers, rice papers or tissue papers, fuse them to a piece of stabilizer or acrylic felt to strengthen and support the stitching.

- Add texture to papers by wrinkling before using.

- This is a great technique for creating quick gifts: Smaller, reinforced, versions make great postcards or greetings, or sandwich paper combinations, such as a birth or wedding announcement and matching ephemera, between layers of organza.

Metal

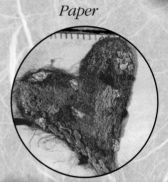

Paper

Journal
10½ x 7¾ inches
Liz Kettle

Transfer Artist Paper
Angelina & Textiva
Thread Painting
Found Objects
Embroidery

Creative Collage
mixed media

For a super creative way to use paper and other unusual elements in your fabric art, try collage. You can pile on the decorative papers and still sew through them!

Dream dreams that no one ever dared to dream before.
Edgar Allan Poe

*Techniques: **Mixed Media**, Printing on Lutradur, Silk Petals, Charms, Silk Cocoons*

mixed media

Non-traditional papers make for non-traditional techniques. Paintable embossed wallpaper, anaglypta, features a treasure trove of motifs and is easy to stitch through. Lutradur is a unique paper-like stabilizer with a translucent quality that can be sewn, printed, stamped and painted, making it a great component for mixed-media work.

supplies

- Assorted papers such as a napkin, anaglypta wallpaper, vellum paper with printed quote.

- Photo or printed image and inkjet printer

- Lutradur

- Acrylic craft or fabric paints

- Acrylic felt

- Fusible web

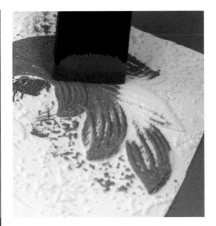

1 Isolate a pretty motif on the wallpaper and cut out with a wide margin. Sponge-brush paint the wallpaper, using multiple layers if desired. Both the red leaf as well as the golden square on this workbook page are painted anaglypta wallpaper motifs.

2 Using the printing on fabric with a label carrier method (page 38), print the image on Lutradur.

3 Fuse a decorative napkin, tissue or rice paper to a piece of acrylic felt with fusible web. If desired, outline-stitch the napkin's pattern elements. Compose the collage elements on the prepared napkin base; stitch the elements in place or choose other attachment methods as previously described. Layer the collage on your fabric base and stitch as desired.

tips

- Paper can add a unique layer of texture not available in fabrics and the array of fabulous papers available is incredible.

- In addition to art papers choose from scrapbook paper, chipboard, Grungeboard, paper flowers, vintage papers, maps, paper bags, shipping tags and don't forget the visual treasures found in magazines and advertising mail.

- Lutradur, although technically not a paper, is strong and yet translucent.

- Fragile tissue and rice papers can be fused to felt or fabric for a unique stitching surface; anaglypta wallpaper bits can be painted and stitched to add exotic patterns to your work.

- Easily color papers with paint, colored pencil, oil pastels or watercolors. While these papers won't hold up to washing, they are suitable for use in decorative fiber projects.

Fabulous & Fun
foam fabrications

Craft foam, generally thought of as a children's product, holds great potential for the inquisitive fiber artist. Among other things, craft foam sheets can be painted, embossed with rubber stamps, and used to create dimensional appliqué motifs with fabric foam forms.

*Techniques: **Foam Fabrications**, Beading, Brads, Couching*

embossed foam

There are no limits to the inventiveness and creativity of fabric artists with a drive to decorate—and even foam cannot escape. The foam sheets are available with or without an adhesive backing and are sometimes available in various thicknesses. For these projects, adhesive-backed thin foam in a riot of colors was used.

supplies

- Craft foam sheets such as Darice Foamies
- Rubber stamps
- Foam paint brushes
- Acrylic craft or fabric paint
- Parchment paper

1 Select a simple rubber stamp with a deeply etched pattern without a lot of fine details. Place the foam, right side up, on your ironing surface and place parchment paper over the foam. Iron the foam until it begins to soften and curl slightly—time will vary depending on your iron but generally takes 10–30 seconds.

2 Quickly remove the iron and parchment and press the rubber stamp very firmly into the warm foam.

3 Remove the stamp and trim the foam as desired. Repeat as many times as desired, using foam in a variety of colors and stamps in a variety of patterns.

4 No special steps are required to prepare the foam for paint. Paint can be used sparingly and multiple layers and colors may be applied. Apply paint with a foam brush. Create several stamped and painted foam pieces in a variety of sizes. When dry, layer and stitch the foam pieces in place.

foam-filled fabric

Combine the heat-shrinking ability of foam with fabric to create dimensional appliqué motifs that jump off the page. Simply encase the foam in fabric, cut out your shape, stitch and heat and, presto, your shape is done.

supplies

- Craft foam sheets—Darice Foamies
- Template plastic
- Marking pencil or pen
- Flower and leaf pattern
- Double stick tape
- Parchment paper
- Heat gun

1 Draw simple flower and leaf patterns on template plastic and cut out. Remove the foam's paper backing and stick a piece of fabric on the adhesive side of the foam. Place another piece of fabric on the front side of the foam, securing it with double-stick tape near the edges. Trace the flower pattern on the fabric.

2 Set your machine for free-motion stitching and stitch on the drawn pattern lines. For thicker lines, stitch the pattern lines twice. Fill the center of each flower with circular stitching and, if desired, add short lines in the petals. Repeat for the leaves.

3 Cut out the flower shapes about ⅛ inch beyond the stitched outlines.

4 Heat the cut-out flowers and leaves with the heat gun until the foam within the fabric begins to shrink and curl slightly. The length of time required to shrink the foam varies with the distance you keep the heat gun. Apply and decorate flowers and leaves as desired.

Not Your Grandmother's Crazy Quilt
17 x 23 inches
Ruth Chandler

Sashiko

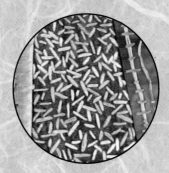

Ricing

*Traditional Crazy Quilting
Embroidery*

139

Storing Treasures
plastic packs

Add treasured keepsakes to a quilt or children's fabric book by placing them in small plastic pockets and enclosed packets.

Techniques: ***Plastic Packs,*** *Stamping, Buttons, Couching*

plastic packs

Add small items to your quilt, such as photos, birth and wedding announcements, programs and ticket stubs or a shipping tag with a collage, without damaging your work. Below, find three options to try.

supplies

- Clear vinyl and/or transparency sheet

- Small elements such as mica flakes, mini glass beads, charms, sequins, beads, buttons, lace, or paper

- Anaglypta wallpaper

- Staz-on ink, rubber stamp

- Item that will be stored in pocket such as a tag

- Clear drying glue

tips

- Plastic tends to slip while being sewn to fabric resulting in a crooked pocket. It is easier to create your treasure packet as a separate element to add to your work later, than to stitch it directly to your work.

- Use masking tape to temporarily secure the plastic while stitching; pins will leave holes.

- Use a longer stitch length than you would for fabric and avoid very dense decorative stitches.

1 Sew a treasure packet directly to your work: First, collect your desired objects. Here, the designer gathered memories of her grandmother—sheet music, a small diary key, a hat feather, and buttons, beads and trim perhaps from her wedding dress?
Cut a piece of vinyl or transparency plastic and place on your work where desired; use masking tape to hold it in place and stitch along the side and bottom edges with a zigzag stitch. Insert your items and stitch the top edge closed. If desired, sew along the edges again with a straight stitch.

2 Make treasure packets as a separate container before adding to your fabric base or create one directly on your fabric. Choose a paper for the base—this example shows a piece of painted anaglypta wallpaper. Cut a piece of clear vinyl slightly larger than the paper base. Layer the vinyl on top of the base and sew along the edges on three sides.
Add the loose elements you wish to encase in your packet—this packet holds a teaspoon of mica flakes. Stitch the remaining side closed. Stitch the piece to the base fabric, sewing slightly away from the previous stitching or use a decorative edge stitch.

3 To make a pocket, cut transparency plastic slightly larger than the item that will

be stored in the pocket plus allow room for stitching and for the item to easily be removed if desired. Use Staz-on stamp ink to stamp an image on the transparency plastic. Place the pocket where desired, hold in place with masking tape, and stitch along three edges with your desired stitch, leaving the top edge open. A small amount of clear glue on the first and last stitches help strengthen them if the item in the pocket will be removed frequently.

Prairie Garden
silk cocoons

Silk cocoons are the actual cocoon created by silk worms—if you reeled off the fibers it could be spun into thread. You need about 250 cocoons to produce one ounce of finished silk! Cocoons can be divided, cut, dyed, painted and sewn.

Techniques: **Cocoons & Rods,** *Beading, Charms*

silk cocoons

Use cocoons just as they are or separate them into layers. Once peeled into layers, you'll find that the inner layer is often a paler color than the outer layer which adds interest to your flowers.

supplies

- Silk cocoons
- Silk carrier rods
- Small disposable container and water
- Craft glue

1 Cut one end off each cocoon (see tips on page 146). Soak the cocoons in water for a few hours to soften the sericin, allowing you to manipulate the cocoon and separate the layers.

2 Once the cocoon has softened you can begin to pry apart an inner layer by gently manipulating the cocoon and gently running your fingernail along the cut edge.

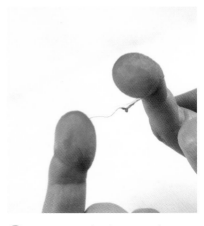

3 Separate the layers with your fingers and continue pulling apart until you have two separate cocoon layers.

POSIES

4 Make several cuts toward the center of the still-wet cocoon, varying the petal width as desired. Splay the petals apart and let dry. Trim the petal ends into an oval shape. To make a flower, off-set two cocoon layers, light on top of dark or vice-versa.

PUFFBALL POD

5 Choose or make a silk carrier rod layer (see steps 1–4 on page 147). Hand-sew a line of running stitches along one edge of the layer. Gently pull the thread to gather the layer. Wrap the thread around the gathered base and knot off. Apply a bit of glue to the base and place in a cocoon.

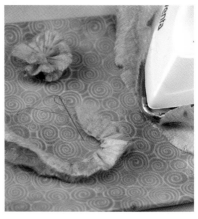

ROSETTE

6 Choose or make a carrier rod layer. Fold the layer in half and press. Thread a hand-sewing needle with a doubled length of cotton thread, knot the end and, using a running stitch, stitch along the folded edge. Gently pull the thread, gathering the layer into a circle. Connect the ends, knot off and clip the thread.

LUPINE

7 Choose or make a layer from a silk carrier rod. Thread a hand-sewing needle with a doubled length of cotton thread. Using a running stitch, sew a zig-zag pattern down the center of the entire layer. Gently pull the thread to gather up the silk, choosing to gather tightly or loosely. Knot the thread and clip.

LEAVES

8 Make six cuts toward the center of the cocoon, not cutting through the end. Let dry. Shape the end of each leaf; splay apart and let dry. Use one entire leaf section behind a flower. Alternatively, cut individual leaves from the cocoon.

STEMS

9 Rip or cut lengths of green fabric in random widths of ¼–½ inch. Ripping the fabric creates frayed edges that add to the texture of your work. Arrange the stems on the base fabric and stitch down the centers with straight stitches. Arrange flowers and leaves and stitch in place as follows: Attach rosettes and posies in the center with a free-motion circular stitch and lupines with a straight stitch along the center. Glue a cocoon end in the center of each posie.

tips

- Silk cocoons vary from dyer to dyer. Some are dyed whole with the silk worm still inside. The advantage of a whole cocoon is you get to determine where to cut open. Some dyers cut the cocoon for you and dispose of the worm. Cutting the cocoon is a simple matter and can be done with scissors or a sharp craft knife.

- Small cocoon ends can be used for flower centers as well as at the very end of silk carrier rods.

- Because cocoons and rods are made of natural fibers they are sometimes misshapen or do not always absorb dye evenly. This can create interesting layers of color and shape variation. Some manufacturers sell cocoons that are more consistent in size if needed for a particular project.

Fuchsia on Silk
14 x 20 inches
Heather Thomas

Thread Lace Appliqué

Underwater World
silk carrier rods

Silk carrier rods often look like split tree branches and are the result of reeling silk cocoon fibers over a rod—excess silk fibers build up on these rods and are cut away. Carrier rods take dye beautifully and have that incredible luster that only silk can give.

Techniques: ***Silk Carrier Rods***, *Wrinkling, Hand Embroidery, Beading*

silk carrier rods

Silk rods contain sericin, a natural gum that holds together the silk fibers, making them quite inflexible. With a little manipulation the rods separate into layers which become wonderful embellishments.

supplies

• Silk carrier rods in assorted colors

• Hand dyed silk organza

• Fabric for background

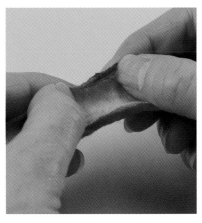

1 Choose a silk carrier rod in a color of your choice and begin to manipulate it with your hands by holding the rod horizontally and gently spreading it open along the split edge with your thumbs.

2 With your fingertips and nails, gently begin to massage the long edges toward the ends, softening the fibers and breaking down the serecin. Do this for a while until the rod is soft and pliable.

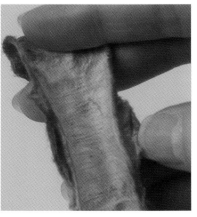

3 You will begin to see fiber layers along the long edges of the split rod; gently manipulate the edge with your thumb nail to separate the layers, working along the entire edge, lifting the thin layers.

4 Each rod can be split into multiple layers and can be left thick or peeled very thin. The layers may not come off in one long piece—be prepared to end up with a variety of lengths.

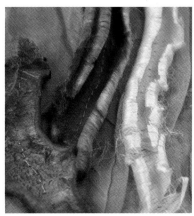

5 Wrinkle the organza and glue to the background fabric. Arrange the rod layers on the organza, allowing them to curl and cup the wrinkles; pin in place. Using matching threads, stitch the rods to the background using a straight stitch in the center of the rod so the edges can curl up.

Scrap Saver fabric beads

Creating beads from fabric is addictive and a most enjoyable way to use up your scraps. Make them in just about any size, using leftover bits of fabric and other goodies you have laying around your work area.

Technique: **Fabric Beads**

fabric beads

Use these wonderful beads to make jewelry, adorn a wall quilt, or design a journal quilt using a few choice beads as the focal point. The possibilities for making and using fabric beads are endless!

supplies

FOR GLUED BEADS
- Variety of fabric scraps
- Fabric glue stick

FOR MELTED BEADS
- Variety of synthetic fabric scraps such as nylon or polyester organza
- Fabrics prepared with Angelina fibers, Textiva film or painted Lutradur
- Straight pins
- Heat gun and respirator

GENERAL
- Fibers and trims
- Glass, metal or wood beads
- Colorful metal wire
- Needle nose pliers with cutter
- Beading thread
- Short dowels in various diameters
- Scissors, rotary cutting tools

GLUED FABRIC BEADS

1 Choose three coordinating fabrics. Cut a 2 x 6-inch strip from one fabric, a 1 x 5-inch strip from a second fabric, and a ¼ x 4-inch strip from a third fabric. Place the widest strip, right side down, on your work surface and rub glue on the entire back except the top 1½ inches which will wrap around the dowel.

2 Center the dowel on the unglued end of the strip and carefully begin rolling the dowel down the strip, being careful to keep the fabric's side edges even as you roll. Keep rolling until the entire fabric strip is rolled around the dowel.

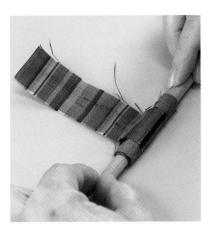

3 Apply glue to the entire back of the second strip and, centering it on the first fabric, roll it around the dowel. Roll the entire strip around the dowel.

Using the same technique add the final, most narrow, strip. For finishing suggestions, refer to Step 8 on page 150.

MELTED FABRIC BEADS

4 These are made similar to the Glued Beads except a heat gun is used to melt the layers together. The fabrics used in this technique need to be synthetic such as polyester or nylon. Painted Lutradur (a synthetic stabilizer) and fabrics made from Angelina and Crystalina fibers, as well as Textiva, can also be used to make melted beads.

Choose 3–4 different fabrics and cut them to the sizes directed in Step 1 on page 149. Wrap the widest strip around the dowel and hold in place.

5 Wrap the next fabric strip around the dowel, centering it on the first strip and, again, hold in place. Apply the third strip.

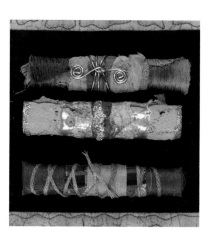

6 Wrap a final length of trim, ribbon, or narrow fabric strip around the dowel, centering it on the third strip and pin through as many layers as possible with a straight pin.

7 Plug in a heat gun and put on your respirator. With the gun set on high heat, direct the heat flow onto the bead, turn the dowel as needed, and carefully watch as the heat melts the layers. Pay attention as you heat the bead and monitor the fabrics. Be careful not to burn through too much fabric or the bead will fall apart.

8 Once the bead has cooled, wrap it with colored wire, thread, ribbon or beads. Remove the dowel, apply glue to the bead ends and dip in glitter or small glass beads, or just ravel the fabric edges.

 tips

- Fabric beads can be made in just about any size. The basic recipe is to have at least two layers, three is better, four is best. Cut the layers in various widths, with the base layer the widest and the final layer the narrowest. Cut the base layer long enough to wrap around the dowel at least 5 times. Wrap subsequent layers around the dowel at least 3 times.

- For a small three-layer bead, sizes are given in Step 1 on page 149. For a slightly larger bead use a ¾-inch diameter dowel and cut 4 x 7-inch, 2 x 6-inch and ½ x 5-inch strips. For a much larger bead, use a 1½-inch diameter dowel, and 6 x 10-, 3½ x 8-, and 2 x 6-inch strips.

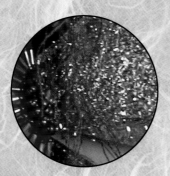

Angelina

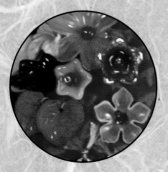

Beading

Stamping
Wool Beads
Foiling
Sequins
Charms

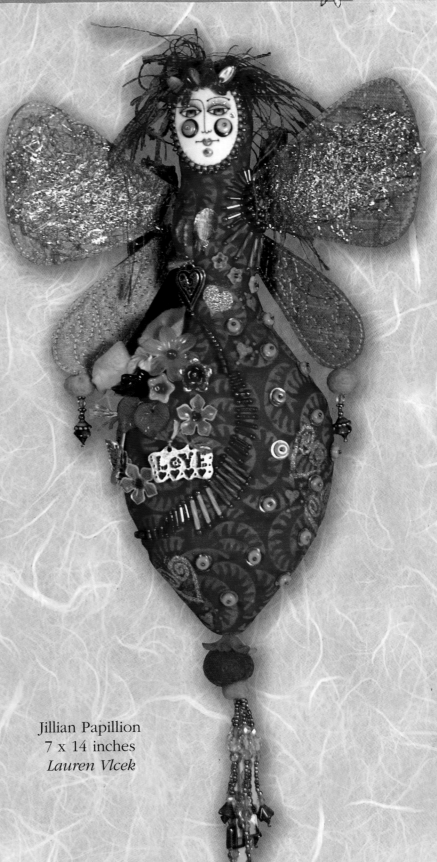

Jillian Papillion
7 x 14 inches
Lauren Vlcek

Flaming Fabric edge burning

This is a wonderful technique to use on art quilts, either directly on the edge of the quilt itself or on a quilted block which is then placed on top of a background. The look can be very old fashioned or quite contemporary.

Techniques: ***Burning***, *Stamping, Iron-on Crystals, Buttons*

edge burning

It is best to burn only those fabrics that you plan never to wash. If washing a burned-edge quilt becomes necessary, wash by hand. You may want to re-burn any areas that fall away during the washing process.

supplies

- Quilted piece made with cotton or other natural fabrics, thin 100% cotton batting and cotton thread.

- Cigarette lighter—if possible choose one without a child safety feature.

- Old cotton towel and an old cotton wash cloth.

tips

- Quilt somewhat heavily along the borders or edges that are to be burned— if the quilting is not close together, it may allow the fire to travel between the quilt layers which can cause one or more layers to burn more rapidly than the others and weaken the edges. Trim away any excess batting or backing before burning.

- Do this technique outside or with open windows—it can get smoky and you don't want your smoke alarms going off.

- It takes a long time for the edge of a quilt to burn. Take your time and never panic!

1 Burn only about six inches of quilt edge at a time. If working on a wall quilt, begin in the middle of one long edge. If working on a block, begin near a corner along one side. Cover your work surface with a dry old towel and wet, then wring out, a wash cloth. Holding the quilt edge over the dry towel, ignite the lighter and move it so the flame touches the edge of the quilt. Do not hold the lighter below the quilt but next to it, just so the flame hits the quilt edge. Hold the lighter in place until the fabric catches fire— about 10 seconds. Move the lighter up the edge and catch the next inch or two on fire. Keep moving the flame up the edge until about six inches are aflame.

caution

- Use only natural fabrics, cotton batting and cotton thread.
- Carefully monitor the burning edge. Don't let any one area burn more than a ½ inch deep.

2 Once the edge has burned as desired, place it on the dry towel and place the wet dish cloth on top of the flaming area to extinguish the flames. Pull the wet cloth away from the edge, pulling away as much ash as possible. Try hard not to wet the un-burned edges next to the burnt edges. Old towels are nearly impossible to light on fire—they are safe for this process.

3 Repeat with the next six inches of edge and continue working your way along all the edges of the quilt or block. Once all of the edges have been burned take a look at the results. If there are any areas that may need more burning, simply reignite them and monitor carefully so they do not get burned too much.

Layered Organza melting and scoring

Adding texture and pattern to fabric with a soldering iron? Why, yes. Similar to accidentally burning a hole in a synthetic fabric with a too-hot iron, you use a heat tool to melt dots and teardrops and score squiggle lines in a stack of layered synthetics.

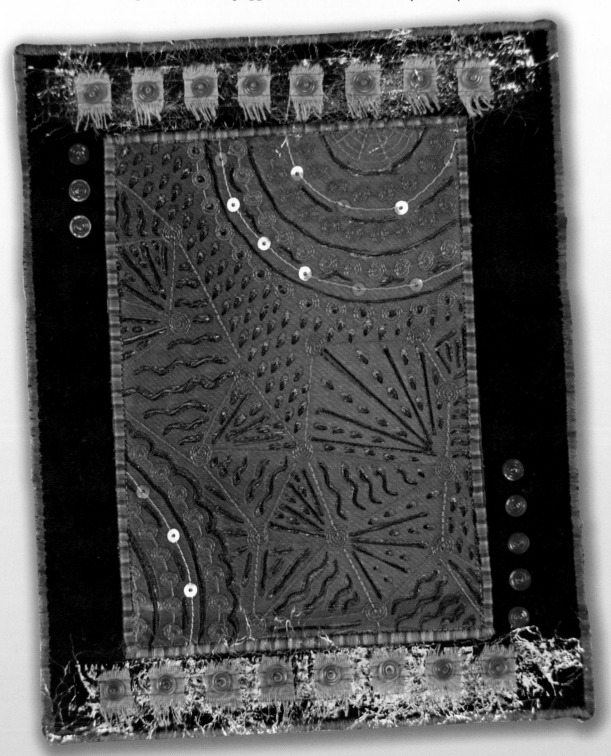

Techniques: **Melting**, *Angelina, Beading*

melting and scoring

The top fabric used here came complete with embroidery and sequins so all you have to do is layer a variety of organzas underneath and then go to work with your burning tool. Aside from your favorite fabric haunts, check the accessories section in department or specialty stores for exotic scarves from India.

supplies

- Selection of synthetic organza and other synthetic fabrics in a variety of colors, solids, multi-colored prints and embroidered or adorned with sparkles and or sequins.

- Very heavy and firm stabilizer such as Peltex or Timtex, the size of the finished piece

- Two pieces of cotton fabric and two pieces of iron-on adhesive, the size of the finished piece

- Straight pins, thread to match or coordinate

- Creative Textile Tool, fine-tipped soldering iron or other fine-tipped burning tool

- Metal ruler or straight edge

- Glass, metal or ceramic surface to work on

- Respirator

1 To prepare the organza layers for the melting process, iron one piece of adhesive to one side of the Timtex or Peltex base; top with a piece of cotton fabric and iron in place. Choose a selection of coordinating organza fabrics. Layer several of these fabrics—the layers can be made from whole pieces of fabric (cut larger than the base) or from chunks and or strips of fabric (cut smaller than the base). However, the final, top layer should be whole and cut larger than the base. As shown here, the top layer is factory embroidered and embellished with sequins. Stack the layers on top of the fabric-side of the Peltex and pin together. With the Peltex/Timtex side up. Straight-stitch all around just inside the edge.

caution

- Melting man-made materials can be caustic, stinky, and give off toxic fumes. This is best done outdoors and should always be done while wearing a respirator.

2 Insert a fine pointed tip into your burning tool, turn it on and allow it to heat up. Set a piece of protective glass, marble or ceramic tile or metal on your work surface. Set your metal ruler near your work area and put on a respirator. Using the burning tool, trim the edges even with the base.

3 To burn off any stray thread ends and to seal the edges, run the heat tool along each trimmed edge.

4 Visually divide the surface into sections—try for an asymmetrical design with diagonal lines rather than a basic grid. If your fabric has a printed or stitched design, try following the design as you section it out. Next, melt a series of marks on the surface of your organza sandwich. Some marks will be long, fine lines, some straight, some curvy, see Step 5. Some marks will be dots or teardrops, see Step 6. Whatever you can 'doodle' with a pencil you can melt with your fine-tipped heat tool. A light touch of the tool will melt through the first layer; the heavier the touch, the more layers you melt through. The cotton layer on the base will act as a resist to help keep from burning the Peltex or Timtex base.

5 For scoring lines, insert the tip and pull it one direction. Deeply inserting the tip and moving it slowly will yield a wide line that will probably penetrate all organza layers while just slightly inserting the tip and moving quickly will melt fewer layers.

6 To melt teardrop shapes, insert the tip, then angle to one side. Leaving the tip inserted for just a second or two will yield a shallow hole while leaving the tip inserted for several seconds may melt through all of the layers. For dots, insert the tip perpendicular to the surface.

- Synthetics burn or melt at differing rates depending on their chemical compounds. Prior to using it in your project, do a test melt on each fabric.

- Pieces worked with this technique make great mailable gifts. Find some fancy envelopes at your local paper store and make mini quilts slightly smaller than the envelope. Pop your mini art work in an envelope and surprise a friend.

7 Once you have completed the melting and scoring, decide if you want to add beads, sequins or charms. Hand-sew them in place following the techniques given elsewhere in this book. Iron the remaining pieces of adhesive and cotton to the back of the base. Load your machine with thread to match or coordinate with your organza and machine quilt a few lines through all of the layers of organza in a design that will accentuate the burned lines. Switch to a satin stitch and finish the edges of the piece. If desired, topstitch the piece to a quilted background.

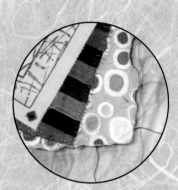

Burned Edges

Sequins

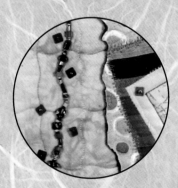

Beading

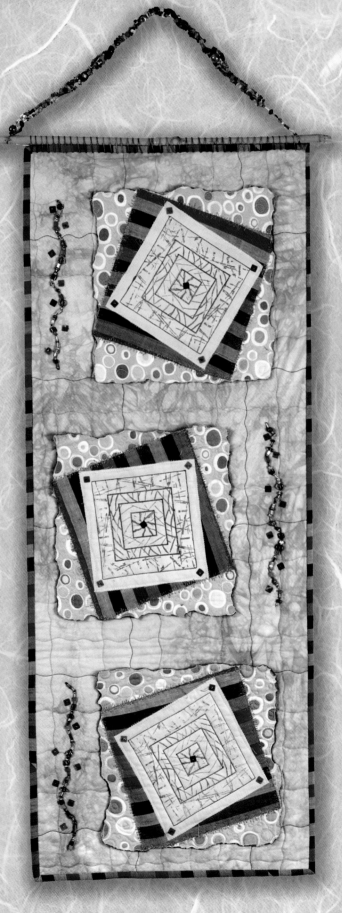

Purple Party
14 x 33 inches
Heather Thomas

Ruth Chandler grew up in Japan where the vibrant color and texture of Japanese fabric combined with the simplicity of Japanese design caught Ruth's attention. Ruth learned basic Sashiko from an elderly neighbor and at the age of 10 she began to create and sew her own clothes which became an outlet for her imagination and creativity.

Ruth made her first quilt in 1990—a queen size hand-appliquéd and hand-quilted Hawaiian pineapple quilt, and she has never looked back. In her own unique style, she loves to use new techniques mingled with the old and her work usually shows the influence of her years spent in Japan.

Ruth lives in Colorado with her very supportive husband of 31 years. She has a daughter and son, both married, and 3 beautiful grandchildren. Ruth may be contacted at ruthachandler@comcast.net.

Liz Kettle is a fabric and mixed media artist with a passion for teaching others the joy of making art and the creative process. After filling her tool box with the skills for success in the traditional quilting arena she began to delve into art quilting and discovered a world of freedom and fun in mixed media.

Liz's eclectic work is influenced by her beautiful surroundings, the foothills of the Rocky Mountains, and her love of vintage textiles and history. She incorporates layers and found objects to tell stories of the land and people. When she isn't creating visual art, Liz writes about creativity and the creative process. She is the founder of Textile Evolution, a unique retreat (www.textileevolution.com).

Liz lives in Colorado with her very supportive husband and three amazing sons who are just beginning their own journeys.

Ruth's Techniques

Weaving Fabric
Tic-Tac-Toe Tucks
Stitches & Bits
Bubbles & Wrinkles
Sashiko
Ricing
Machine Couching
Mini Marbles

Liz's Techniques

Inkjet Printing
Printing on Lutradur
Printing on Ribbon
Photo Transfer
Thread-Lace Grid
Thread-Lace
Appliqué
Thread Painting
Needle Felting

Make Mine Metal
Embossed Metal
Attaching Paper
Nine-Patch Sampler
Mixed Media
Foam Fabrications
Plastic Packs
Silk Cocoons
Silk Carrier Rods

Heather Thomas began quilting over 23 years ago, taking a turn toward art quilting around the year 2000. She self-publishes her line of more than 100 patterns under the name Wild Heather Designs. She has been teaching her designs and techniques for over 15 years and, for the past 10 years, has taught a 13-month color and design class during which she has worked with more than 2,000 aspiring artists.

Creating art is Heather's driving force, her reason for being here, her love and her passion. It is her hope to inspire her students to creative freedom and help them discover their possibilities.

Heather is the mother of two grown girls and married Tom, her new best friend, in the summer of 2007. She and her husband own a quilt shop, Wild Heather, in Englewood, Colorado and an internet store, wildheatherdesigns.com.

Heather Thomas, Artist, Publisher, Writer, Designer, Instructor 3431 S. Broadway, Englewood CO 80113

Lauren Vlcek, an accomplished artist and doll maker, has been creating and selling one-of-a-kind works of art for over fifteen years. Her unique talent and years of experience have culminated in inspiring fiber/mixed media art works.

Lauren's often whimsical creations encompass unique design, confluence of color, extensive bead work, surprising attention to detail and are an exploration of spirit, imagination and self. She wishes to educate people on contemporary fiber art and create an awareness of techniques in this emerging art medium.

Lauren has displayed her work in art shows, doll challenges, magazine and book covers and on television. For over ten years, she has taught art classes in figurative art and embellishment.

Lauren lives in Colorado Springs, Colorado with her husband and two sons.

Lauren's Techniques

Traditional Crazy Quilting	Wool Beads & Silk Petals
Deconstructed Crazy Quilting	Beads Galore
Fashion a Frame	Sequins, Charms & More
Machine Embroidery - Programmed Stitches	Iron-on Crystals
Rusting Fabric	Decorative Brads

Heather's Techniques

Rubber Stamping	Fabric Foiling
Discharge Dyeing	Going for Glitter
Dévoré or Burn-out	Dimensional Appliqué
Angelina, Textiva and Crystalina	Fabric Beads
	Edge Burning
Tyvek Transformation	Melting and Scoring

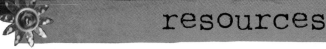

Embellishers are always on the hunt for interesting products and items. Thrift stores and yard sales yield incredible finds and a walk in our neighborhood gives us feathers, stones and tidbits. A visit to the hardware store becomes a treasure hunt for interesting things to add to our collection. Be on the lookout for items you can up-cycle or repurpose. Many products and tools used for embellishing are available at major craft, sewing and quilt stores. Here's a list of our favorite internet stores that feature some of the unique products we love to use:

Internet stores carrying most of the embellishment materials:
Artistic Artifacts: www.artisticartifacts.com
Fiber on a Whim: www.fiberonawhim.com
Joggles.com: www.joggles.com
Wild Heather: www.wildheatherdesigns.com

Internet stores specializing in beads and charms:
Artgirlz: www.artgirlz.com
Beyond Beadery: www.beyondbeadery.com
Cartwright Sequins: www.ccartwright.com
Ey Embellishments: www.eyembellishments.com/store/
Fire Mountain Gems: www.firemountaingems.com
The Bead Corner: www.beadcorneronline.com

Additional great internet resources:
Artemis Inc.: www.artemisinc.com. Hand dyed silk ribbons and trims.
Dharma Trading: www.dharmatrading.com. Discharge paste, fabric prepared for inkjet printing, Fiber Etch, foils and adhesives, hot fix crystals, stamp-carving tools, textile paints.
Dick Blick: www.dickblick.com. Aamco metal sheets and metal mesh, Jacquard fabric for inkjet printing, stamp-carving tools and supplies, textile paints.
Dollmakers Ink: www.dollmakersink.com. Angelina, beads and charms, felt beads, felting needles and fibers, silk cocoons and carrier rods.
Embellishment Village: www.embellishmentvillage.com. Angelina, beads, charms and sequins, foils and adhesives, glitter.
Try Our Designs: www.tryourdesigns.com. Angelina, hot fix crystals, needle felting supplies and fibers, silk carrier rods.
Creative Impressions: www.creativeimpressions.com. Brads, ribbons, stamps and other fun embellishments.
Quilting Arts: www.interweavestore.com/Quilting/Merchandise.html